MW00633275

Teaching Activities Manual for

Break Through!

The **Bible** for **Young Catholics**

Getting to **Know Jesus**

Teaching Activities Manual for

Break Through!

The **Bible** for **Young Catholics**

Getting to **Know Jesus**

Rick Keller-Scholz and Jeannie Pomanowski
with Christine Schmertz Navarro

Saint Mary's Press®

Dedication

This project is dedicated to all of the faith-filled women and men across North America who work with young adolescents in Catholic grade schools and parishes. Thank you.

The publishing team included Christine Schmertz Navarro, development editor; Lorraine Kilmartin, reviewer; Mary Koehler, permissions editor; FaithClipart, image, page 71; prepress and manufacturing coordinated by the production departments of Saint Mary's Press.

Printed in the United States of America

4339

ISBN 978-0-88489-979-2

About Our Principal Authors

Rick Keller-Scholz has spent over twenty years teaching at Bellarmine Preparatory School in Tacoma, WA, and more than ten years as a volunteer junior high parish minister. Rick also teaches in the Archdiocese of Seattle Catechetical Certification Program.

Rick has been awarded "Catechist of the Year" from the Seattle Archdiocese and the Elizabeth Ann Kelley Teacher of the Year award from Bellarmine. He is a contributing author to *Pride in Our Past / Faith in Our Future: Catholic Northwest History Curriculum* (Archives of the Archdiocese of Seattle and the Catholic School's Department [Seattle: Archdiocese of Seattle, 1999]), the *Teaching Activities Manual for "The Catholic Youth Bible®"* (Saint Mary's Press, 2000), and the *Teaching Activities Manual for "Breakthrough! The Bible for Young Catholics": An Introduction to People of Faith* (Saint Mary's Press, 2006).

Rick and his wife, Nancy, live in Tacoma and have three children.

Jeannie Pomanowski has been teaching in Catholic schools for many years and has been teaching middle school religion for the last seven years at Saint Leo the Great School in Lincroft, NJ. In 1999, the Diocese of Trenton awarded Jeannie the "Catholic Educator of the Year" award.

Jeannie is also a songwriter, singer, and recording artist of Christian pop and rock music and has released two albums, *Faith with an Attitude* and *Prayer Warrior,* both published by Be Attitude Music, BMI. Jeannie performs around the country and has shared her skill at the 2001, 2003, and 2005 National Catholic Youth Conference, in addition to other gatherings.

Jeannie is also a principal author for the *Teaching Activities Manual for "Breakthrough! The Bible for Young Catholics": An Introduction to People of Faith* (Saint Mary's Press, 2006).

Christine Schmertz Navarro is a development editor at Saint Mary's Press, having taught several years in high schools and spent volunteer time with young adolescents. She is the principal author of the *Teaching Activities Manual for "The Catholic Youth Bible"* (2000), coauthor of the *Teaching Manual for "Living Justice and Peace: Catholic Social Teaching in Action"* (2001), and editor of several other books, all published by Saint Mary's Press.

Christine and her husband, Rudy, live in Tacoma, WA, and have a nine-year-old daughter.

Contents

Appendices

Introduction

Getting to Know *Breakthrough! The Bible for Young Catholics*, Its Teaching Manual, and Its Student Workbook

Breakthrough! The Bible for Young Catholics has a growing family of resources that complement one another. This teaching manual, *Getting to Know Jesus*, follows the manual subtitled *An Introduction to People of Faith*. Student workbooks accompany both manuals.

The *Breakthrough!* Family of Resources

Breakthrough! The Bible for Young Catholics

Breakthrough! The Bible for Young Catholics will be your strongest resource for introducing young adolescents to the Scriptures. Every element of this Bible was carefully chosen or created to appeal to young people who are ten to thirteen years old. This starts with the choice of using the Catholic Edition of the *Good News Translation* for the Bible text. The *Good News Translation* was created with a vocabulary and reading level appropriate to the younger student. If you have been using translations with a more advanced reading level, you will notice an immediate difference in your students' ability to read and understand the Bible text.

Additionally, *Breakthrough!* provides many other tools to help young people feel more comfortable and familiar with the Bible. Forty illustrated color inserts feature "interviews" with the biblical characters. These character interviews quickly identify the important events in the biblical characters' stories and the roles these people played in salvation history. A four-page salvation history time line at the beginning of the Bible shows how these biblical characters fit into God's big picture of salvation history.

Another key feature is the inclusion of Pray It! Study It! Live It! and Catholic Connection articles. These articles appear alongside the biblical text in forty biblical books. The forty books were chosen to provide the best overview of salvation history and a representative sampling of the different types of books found in the Bible. For these forty books, the articles provide a commentary to help young readers better understand and apply the biblical message to their lives. Pray It! articles give the young readers ideas about applying the spirituality of the Bible. Study It! articles give them background so that they better understand the context of the passages they are reading. Live It! articles challenge the young people to live biblical values and teachings. Catholic Connections articles show where important Catholic teachings are found in the Scriptures.

Some of the other features you will find in *Breakthrough!* are these:

- a complete list of the Sunday readings
- lists to help find important Bible stories, prayers, and teachings
- a word list with definitions of over 180 important Bible words
- nine color maps

The Teaching Manuals and the Bible

The *Teaching Activities Manual for "Breakthrough! The Bible for Young Catholics": An Introduction to People of Faith* (Saint Mary's Press, 2006) provides you with tools to invite young adolescents to encounter God through over forty biblical characters from both the Old and New Testaments. Using a format similar to this manual, the *People of Faith* manual helps you identify similarities between the biblical characters and your students' lives and gives you ideas about how to best introduce the biblical characters to your students in ways that are relevant and interesting.

The *Student Activity Workbook for "Breakthrough! The Bible for Young Catholics": Getting to Know Jesus* (Saint Mary's Press, 2007) invites you to take a similarly personal approach in your study of Jesus. *Getting to Know Jesus* helps you teach about Jesus through his different gifts and experiences. The manual identifies similarities between the lives of Jesus and your students, providing you with options for inviting them into his story and message.

The Teaching Manuals and the Student Workbooks

Both of the manuals have student workbooks that provide the students with ways to learn about a biblical character or Jesus with greater independence. The workbooks have word puzzles to help the students gain familiarity with the content of relevant readings as well as introductions to the subject matter, lists of relevant Scripture passages and "*Breakthrough!*" articles, and questions and space for reflection.

The teaching manual was written to help teachers use the Bible with young people rather than as a guide to using the workbook. This manual does, however, also provide suggestions about ways you can use all three resources together. The workbook puzzles often function like the "Getting to Know the Story of Jesus" activities in that they require the students to read some of the passages they need to be familiar with in order to get to know Jesus better. When you see the workbook icon, you will find suggestions about using the puzzles in conjunction with these activities.

The introductory paragraphs and reflection questions in the workbook often come from the "Getting to Know Jesus" activities. When you see the workbook icon in this section of the teaching activities manual chapters, you will encounter suggestions about when and how you might have students answer the questions in the workbook to enhance their experience of the activities.

The teaching manual and the student workbook both stand alone, however. There are advantages to using them together, but every activity in this manual can be conducted without the workbook, and every activity page in the workbook can be completed without the teaching manual. The needs of your students and your own resources should determine which combination of these products you choose.

About the Term *Young Adolescent*

You will notice that the *Breakthrough!* materials use the term *young adolescent* throughout. This term describes young people of the ages that would normally put them in grades five through eight. We intentionally use a term that describes their age rather than their status in school, which is what would happen if we used *junior high* or *middle school.* We all know that, depending on what part of the country, state, or county you find yourself, even these terms are fluid!

We also use the terms *young people* and *student* to refer to this same group. Even though some activities may lend themselves more readily to the classroom of a Catholic grade school, the authors wrote with both school and parish needs in mind.

Looking More Closely at This Teaching Manual

This teaching manual has many features that will help you in your ministry with young adolescents. Though the Bible itself is not a "curriculum," nor does the teaching manual provide a comprehensive curriculum for biblical study, you will find that this manual will supplement the Christology or New Testament curriculum you are currently using.

This book consists of twelve chapters and three appendices. You can use the chapters in order or pick and choose as you need. In addition to inviting students to learn the stories about Jesus, the material in the chapters enables you to make connections between your young people's lives and the life of Jesus.

The next sections explain the rationale behind the different parts of the chapters.

Preparing to Teach

Each chapter begins with a section called "Preparing to Teach." There is quite a bit of "raw material" in the first half of each chapter, such as Scripture citations, lists of *Breakthrough!* articles, and connections between Jesus and young people. These tools are present to make it easier for you to reflect about your own students and their needs and questions, and then to move quickly into a lesson or session plan that will bring the Bible and its people alive for your young people.

Instead of going through the chapters sequentially, we hope you will make decisions about what and how to teach based on a combination of factors, such as what materials you have and what you think will excite your students. The chapters in this manual are set up to support your own discernment in teaching. Pray about your students' needs, and focus on the aspects of Jesus' life with which they would most identify right now.

The following parts of the chapters should help you tailor your teaching to the needs of your students.

Overview

The overview consists of several paragraphs that bring the chapter topic into focus and highlight ways the subject connects with the young people at their own stage of development.

This Chapter at a Glance

This short section gives you the names of the activities that are in the second half of the chapter. You will see here that each chapter provides at least one activity that helps the young people learn the stories of Jesus and one that helps them probe more deeply into the person of Jesus.

Scripture Passages Related to the Story of Jesus

This section lists no more than twelve key passages about the aspect of Jesus under study. An asterisk identifies those passages that are most important to read. This section should make it easier for you to find relevant passages and to assign reading to your group.

Articles from *Breakthrough!* Related to Jesus

This section lists several articles from *Breakthrough!* that are relevant to your study. The Bible features Pray It! Study It! Live It! articles so that the students can learn more about aspects of the Bible, develop their prayer life, and hear challenges to live differently. These three types of articles as well as the Catholic Connections can be springboards for conversation with your students. When you see the *Breakthrough!* icon in the margin, you will know that you will be directed to an aspect of *Breakthrough! The Bible for Young Catholics.*

Break Through!

Jesus and Young Adolescents Today

This section suggests several connections between Jesus, his ministry, and the young people with whom you are working. Perhaps one or two of the connections will intuitively or obviously seem more suitable for your group now. But next year, with another group, another two may emerge as important.

Activities

The second half of each chapter is devoted to class or session activities. Each chapter has between one and four activities for you to choose from as you explore the person of Jesus with the young people. You will notice that the authors of this manual believe it is possible to learn about Jesus while having an enjoyable, meaningful, and creative time.

There are two types of activities in each chapter:

- **Getting to Know the Story of Jesus.** This activity exposes the young people to the *story* of Jesus either by inviting the young people to read the Scripture passages themselves or by sharing this task with their peers.
- **Getting to Know Jesus.** This activity presumes that the students know the stories about Jesus for the chapter. The activities explore *who Jesus is* and make connections between Jesus, his ministry, and the young people's own life experiences. These activities are more reflective and invite group discussion.

The Appendices: Making It Easier for You

Appendix 1: Additional Resources

This appendix suggests resources that provide background for you and materials that can help you share the beauty of the Scriptures with the students.

Appendix 2: Answer Key for *Breakthrough!* Workbook Puzzles

This appendix contains the answers for the word puzzles that appear in the *Student Activity Workbook for "Breakthrough! The Bible for Young Catholics"*: *Getting to Know Jesus.* This appendix does not directly connect with any materials in this teaching manual. You may choose to use the student workbook to give your students additional opportunities to learn about Jesus and his story. The workbook is available from Saint Mary's Press, *www.smp.org.*

Appendix 3: Index of Activities by Chapter

This appendix lists the activities from the manual by chapter, enabling you to quickly find them and providing you with some sense of the learning styles and methods they use.

Journeying with the Young People

Early adolescence is an exciting age from which to be looking at the stories and person of Jesus. Young people are fairly preoccupied with the opportunities, experiences, and turmoil of this age, so they are primed for stories about Jesus that speak of trying new things, relating with friends, making a difference, wrestling with rejection, and making important decisions.

The opportunity to look at these issues in light of Jesus' life presents young people with a model of how to address the issues in a loving way, with prayer and grace, and in Christian community. These young people are continuing to transition into an adult faith and relationship with Jesus. You have the privilege to journey with them.

Chapter 1

Getting to Know Jesus and His Family

Preparing to Teach

Overview

Jesus was born into and grew up in a family. Although his childhood and young adolescence are centuries and thousands of miles away, young people can come to understand that they themselves share many human experiences with Jesus. It helps young people to realize that Mary is likely about their age when the angel appears to her and that the story of Jesus in the Temple probably happened when he was a young adolescent. Our students and their parents are not the only ones who miscommunicate!

Mary, Joseph, and Jesus are a model loving family. Jesus learns a humble trade and participates in the religious rituals of a devout Jewish family. It would be a mistake, however, to idealize that this family had it easy by any means. They faced homelessness, became refugees in another country, and likely lived a subsistence lifestyle. Students can see that it was not always Christmas for this family, even though that is a snapshot of their family life that we tend to focus on.

This Chapter at a Glance

Getting to Know the Story of Jesus and His Family

- The Birth of Jesus

Getting to Know Jesus and His Family

- *Las Posadas*
- Jesus and Human Rights Violations

Scripture Passages Related to Jesus and His Family

The passages listed in bold are readings the students will reference to complete the puzzle “Jesus and His Family” on page 9 of the *Student Activity Workbook for “Breakthrough! The Bible for Young Catholics”: Getting to Know Jesus.*

- **Matthew 1:1–17** (The ancestors of Jesus Christ)
- **Luke 2:1–7, Matthew 1:18–25** (The birth of Jesus Christ)*
- **Luke 2:8–20** (The shepherds and the angels)*
- **Matthew 2:1–12** (Visitors from the East)*
- **Matthew 2:13–15** (The escape to Egypt)
- **Luke 2:21** (Jesus is named.)
- **Matthew 2:16–18** (The killing of the children)
- **Matthew 2:19–23** (The return from Egypt)
- **Luke 2:39–40** (The return to Nazareth)
- **Luke 2:22–38** (Jesus is presented in the Temple.)*
- **Luke 2:41–52** (The boy Jesus in the Temple)*

Asterisk (*) signifies key passages to cover.

Articles from *Breakthrough!* Related to Jesus and His Family

- King of Kings (Matthew 1:1-17)
- Remember Moses? (Matthew 2:13-18)
- “Born of the Virgin Mary” (Luke 1:26-38)
- Hail Mary! (Luke 1:41-42)
- “Where Were You?” (Luke 2:41-51)

Jesus’ Family and Young Adolescents Today

- Jesus is fully human. Adolescents share in Christ’s human nature.
- The facts surrounding the birth of Jesus were rather scandalous. Some students were also born under circumstances that others may have considered less than ideal.
- Joseph and Mary were poor. Many young adolescents can relate to a life of frugality.
- Jesus’ birth brought visitors from afar. The birth of each student brought with it a celebration and visits from relatives and friends.
- Jesus, Mary, and Joseph are refugees from violence. Young adolescents are aware of people seeking refuge because of violence in their communities.

- Jesus and his parents did not communicate well about their plans to leave Jerusalem. Young people and their parents can miscommunicate at times.
- Jesus did not see eye to eye with Mary about being by himself in the Temple. Young adolescents and their parents do not always agree on how much freedom young people should have.

Getting to Know the Story of Jesus and His Family

The Birth of Jesus

In this activity the young adolescents read an excerpt from Luke, chapter 2 in order to review or learn the main events surrounding Jesus' birth.

If the students are using the workbook, they can work on the puzzle "Jesus and His Family" on page 9, which covers not only Luke's narrative but Matthew's also. The activity on handout 1-A, "The Birth of Jesus," prepares students for puzzle questions about Luke. See appendix 2 of this manual for the solution to the puzzle.

Preparation

- ❑ Make copies of handout 1-A, "The Birth of Jesus," one for each student.
- ❑ Complete the handout yourself before meeting with the students.
- ❑ Provide each young person with a copy of *Breakthrough! The Bible for Young Catholics* or another Bible and a pen or pencil.

1. Give each student a copy of handout 1-A, "The Birth of Jesus," a Bible, and a pen or pencil. Ask the young people to read Luke 2:1-12 quietly to themselves. When they finish reading, ask them to close their bibles and fill in the handout from memory.

2. When all the students are done with the handout, have them self-check their work by opening their bibles to the passage in Luke and reviewing their answers. Call on students to share their answers with the class. Answer any questions they might have about the reading.

Getting to Know Jesus and His Family

Las Posadas

"Las Posadas" is a wonderful Advent activity that involves the whole school or religious education program. In this activity the students recreate the journey from Nazareth to Bethlehem in the Mexican tradition of *Las Posadas.* Because this activity ideally involves schoolwide participation, it is important to give advance notice and directives to all involved.

Preparation

- ❑ Have the class create invitations for all the other classes in the school, inviting them to *Las Posadas.* Let the classes know they will each have to assign one student as their innkeeper.
- ❑ Have your students include a short explanation of the Mexican tradition of *Las Posadas.* (Information about this celebration is readily available on the Internet.)
- ❑ *Las Posadas* is a Mexican tradition. *Las Posadas* means "inn" and "to find a safe place." The celebration is a re-enactment of the arrival of Joseph and Mary in Bethlehem. Ask each class in the school to decide on a name for their inn and decorate their classroom door.

1. Assign two students in your class to play the roles of Mary and Joseph.

2. On the designated day, begin *Las Posadas* with your class. Instruct Mary and Joseph to knock at each classroom door that is decorated. The townspeople (the remaining members of your class) follow Mary and Joseph from inn (classroom) to inn. Have the designated innkeepers from each class turn them away. Once a class's innkeeper has turned away Mary and Joseph, that whole class, including the innkeeper, should join the procession.

3. When Mary and Joseph reach the last inn and are again turned away, they then lead the whole school community to assemble in the sanctuary or auditorium to sing appropriate Advent or Christmas hymns, such as "O Holy Night" or "Away in a Manger."

4. Lead the students in a discussion of their experience of *Las Posadas.* What did it feel like to play the different roles of innkeeper, Mary, Joseph, and the townspeople?

Additional suggestion. Play instrumental Advent or Christmas hymns quietly over the public address system while Mary and Joseph go from inn to inn. Remind all students to remain silent during the procession so as to present a solemn, holy environment for the event.

Jesus and Human Rights Violations

In this activity the students study several events in Jesus' life from the perspective of current international law in order to reflect more deeply on the story of his early years.

Preparation

- ❑ Make copies of handouts 1-B, "Human Rights," and 1-C, "Human Rights and the Life of Jesus," one of each for each student.
- ❑ Reflect on or research human rights issues. The United Nations has a helpful Web site for teachers.

1. Pass out handout 1-B, "Human Rights," and go through the articles with the students. Clarify any questions they might have about the language used in the articles.

2. Discuss the importance of these articles in the global community. If there are any issues of human rights in the news, refer to them or to past events the students would be familiar with, to help illustrate the articles.

3. Distribute handout 1-C, "Human Rights and the Life of Jesus," and ask the young people to complete it individually, using handout 1-B as a reference. Discuss the results as a class. Ask the students how they think the experience of having their human rights violated shaped Jesus and his parents.

4. If your students have the workbook, this would be a good time for them to answer question 1 on page 10, which asks them to find similarities between their own birth and Jesus' birth. Have them answer the question in writing.

The Birth of Jesus

At the time Emperor ______________ ordered a ______________ to be taken throughout the ______________ Empire. . . . Everyone, then, went to register himself, each to his own hometown. Joseph went from the town of ______________ in Galilee to the town of ______________ in Judea, the birthplace of King David. . . . He went to register with ________________, who was promised in marriage to him. She was pregnant, and while they were in ______________, the time came for her to have her baby. She gave birth to her first son, wrapped him in cloths and laid him in a ______________—there was no room for them to stay in the ______________.

There were some ______________ in that part of the country who were spending the night in the fields, taking care of their flocks. An ______________ of the Lord appeared to them, and the glory of the Lord shone over them. They were terribly afraid, but the angel said to them, "Don't be ______________! I am here with ______________ for you, which will bring great joy to all people. This very day in David's town your Savior was born—Christ the Lord!" (Luke 2:1,3–12)

Human Rights

*From the "Universal Declaration of Human Rights"	**Convention on the Rights of the Child
Article 3. Everyone has the right to life, liberty and security of person.	Article 6 1. States Parties recognize that every child has the inherent right to life. 2. States Parties shall ensure to the maximum extent possible the survival and development of the child.
Article 13. 2. Everyone has the right to leave any country, including his own, and to return to his country.	Article 10 2. A child whose parents reside in different States shall have the right to maintain on a regular basis, save in exceptional circumstances, personal relations and direct contacts with both parents. Towards that end and in accordance with the obligation of States Parties under article 9, paragraph 1, States Parties shall respect the right of the child and his or her parents to leave any country, including their own, and to enter their own country. The right to leave any country shall be subject only to such restrictions as are prescribed by law and which are necessary to protect the national security, public order (ordre public), public health or morals or the rights and freedoms of others and are consistent with the other rights recognized in the present Convention.
Article 14. 1. Everyone has the right to seek and to enjoy in other countries asylum from persecution.	Article 22 1. States Parties shall take appropriate measures to ensure that a child who is seeking refugee status or who is considered a refugee in accordance with applicable international or domestic law and procedures shall, whether unaccompanied or accompanied by his or her parents or by any other person, receive appropriate protection and humanitarian assistance in the enjoyment of applicable rights set forth in the present Convention and in other international human rights or humanitarian instruments to which the said States are Parties.
Article 16. 3. The family is the natural and fundamental group unit of society and is entitled to protection by society and the State.	
Article 25. 2. Motherhood and childhood are entitled to special care and assistance. All children, whether born in or out of wedlock, shall enjoy the same social protection.	

*(Articles from "Universal Declaration of Human Rights," on the United Nations' Web site. Used with permission.)
**(Articles from "United Nations Convention on the Rights of the Child," on the United Nations' Web site. Used with permission.)

Human Rights and the Life of Jesus

Match the events in Jesus' life with the articles from the United Nations, which crafted these documents in the last century.

The circumstances surrounding the consequent birth of Jesus were rather scandalous because Mary and Joseph were betrothed to be married when Mary became pregnant by the power of the Holy Spirit.

____

"After they had left, an angel of the Lord appeared in a dream to Joseph and said, 'Herod will be looking for the child in order to kill him. So get up, take the child and his mother and escape to Egypt, and stay there until I tell you to leave.'" (Matthew 2:13)

____

"When Herod realized that the visitors from the East had tricked him, he was furious. He gave orders to kill all the boys in Bethlehem and its neighborhood who were two years old and younger." (Matthew 2:16)

____

Chapter 2

Getting to Know Jesus' Baptism and Temptation

Preparing to Teach

Overview

Many young people have been baptized, whether in the Catholic Church or in another Christian denomination. All of them have been tempted to sin. It is interesting that Jesus is sent by the Holy Spirit into the desert right after his baptism. The proximity of the two stories suggests how much the grace of baptism is needed to resist temptation. Though young people may not be thinking daily about their Baptism, they need to know that they have a special character because of it, one that has the strength to resist temptation if it is not weakened significantly by sin.

At Jesus' baptism God the Father affirms Jesus in his truest identity as God's Son. Then, in the desert, Jesus confronts those forces that seek to corrupt this identity and destiny. Many adults experience both reinforcement and doubt about their true identity, but young adolescents can perceive it to be an overwhelming struggle at times.

The young adolescent is very sensitive to the importance of belonging—being "the beloved," "the special one"—and may believe that association with a certain group or team can provide the status they desire, at least for a short time. Yet this status often remains elusive; the feeling of being "the unbeloved" or "the ordinary one" can weigh on the young student.

Like Jesus the young adolescent's sense of true self is challenged. Young adolescent believers struggle with social acceptance and are tempted to compromise their integrity to simply avoid the hassle of defending their faith. This chapter can help the students recognize their true selves, as Jesus did, and also provide them with tools to reject those voices that would cause them to doubt God's care for them and that would try to persuade them that they are foolish to want to serve others so willingly.

This Chapter at a Glance

Getting to Know the Story of Jesus' Baptism and Temptation

- Presentations of Baptism and Temptation

Getting to Know Jesus Through His Baptism and Temptation

- Baptism: Path to Our True Identity
- Resisting the Tempter with Jesus Today

Scripture Passages Related to Jesus' Baptism and Temptation

The passages listed in bold are readings the students will reference to complete the puzzle "Jesus' Baptism and Temptation" on page 11 of the *Student Activity Workbook for "Breakthrough! The Bible for Young Catholics": Getting to Know Jesus.*

- Matthew 3:13-17, **Mark 1:9–11**, Luke 3:21-22 (The baptism of Jesus)*
- **Matthew 4:1–11**, Mark 1:12-13, Luke 4:1-13 (The temptation of Jesus)*
- Matthew 16:21-28, **Mark 8:31–33**, Luke 9:22-27 (Jesus speaks about his suffering and death.)
- **Mark 9:42–47**, Matthew 18:6-9 (Temptations to sin)
- **Mark 10:35–45** (The request of James and John)
- Matthew 28:16-20, Mark 16:14-18, Luke 24:36-49 (Jesus appears to his disciples.)*

Asterisk (*) signifies key passages to cover.

Break Through!

Articles from *Breakthrough!* Related to Jesus' Baptism and Temptation

- Facing the Devil (Matthew 4:1-11)
- Lent (Mark 1:12-13)
- Baptism, Born Again! (John 3:1-8)

Jesus' Baptism and Temptation and Young Adolescents Today

- The baptism of Jesus marks the beginning of his public ministry and shows all that he is beloved by God. Though many young adolescents may not remember their own Baptism, they can realize that they too are beloved of God and that because of their Baptism, God has a ministry for them to do.

- Jesus is willing to commit his life to God out of total love and says that his future suffering will be a baptism. Jesus' suffering, death, and Resurrection bring life. Young people can see that the Paschal mystery allows people to grow through their suffering if they take it to God.
- Jesus experiences the pull of temptation as do young adolescents. Jesus is a model of resisting temptation and not giving in to selfishness.
- The devil tempts Jesus to use his gifts selfishly. Young adolescents face similar temptations.

Getting to Know the Story of Jesus' Baptism and Temptation

Presentations of Baptism and Temptation

Preparation

❑ Provide copies of *Breakthrough! The Bible for Young Catholics* or another Bible, one for each student.

1. Distribute the bibles. Then divide the class into six groups and assign each group one of the readings from "Scripture Passages Related to Jesus' Baptism and Temptation." Ask the students to read their passages individually in silence and then aloud in the group.

2. These readings contain quite a bit of imagery. Ask each group to create either a still-life representation of the reading or a skit about it. Once a group has presented its visual presentation of the story, ask the members to share what they learned either about Baptism or temptation from their reading. If you review these readings later, the students can perform again to help the group remember the stories.

If your students have workbooks, they can now assess their knowledge of these stories by completing the "Jesus' Baptism and Temptation" puzzle on page 11. See appendix 2 of this manual for the solution to the puzzle.

Getting to Know Jesus Through His Baptism and Temptation

Baptism: Path to Our True Identity

Preparation

- ❑ Provide each student with a copy of *Breakthrough! The Bible for Young Catholics* or another Bible, a pen or pencil, and a sheet of paper.
- ❑ Gather the following additional supplies for this activity:
  - a white board and marker for notes
  - a clear drinking glass
  - two cups of milk
  - a can opener
  - a can of chocolate syrup

1. Introduce this activity by reminding the young people that during Jesus' baptism, God the Father reveals himself and his love to Jesus and that this love is central to Jesus' identity as well as his mission. Divide the class into three small groups. Assign each of the three groups one of the different accounts of Jesus' baptism (Matthew 3:3–17, Mark 1:9–11, Luke 3:21–22) and compare the accounts together as a whole class.

2. Ask the young people to reflect on these two questions:

- ❍ What do you think your identity is based on?
- ❍ How can you grow in knowing your own true identity as God's beloved?

The young people may respond in several ways. Part of their sense of identity comes from looking back on their personal histories through scrapbooks, pictures, and stories. They also learn who they are through their interactions with family and friends. Ask the young people these questions:

- ❍ What is identity theft?
- ❍ What must be scary about identity theft?
- ❍ What kinds of things must people do to "recapture" their stolen identity?

Share these thoughts with the students in your own words:

- ❍ So much deeper than our identity, according to the United States government (and even our scrapbooks), is our identity in God. Each one of us is made in God's image before Baptism. In Baptism, however, we become members of Christ. We are incorporated in the Catholic Church and take on the mission of the Catholic Church. This identity is much closer to the identity we feel within our own families.

3. Note that when we ally ourselves with a sports team or an important cause, we incorporate this sports team or cause into our identity. Ask the young people these questions:

- What are some of the differences between die-hard sports team fans and casual followers of a sports team?
- What might a die-hard follower of Jesus look like? What might a casual follower of Jesus look like?

Share these thoughts with your students in your own words:

- When adults enter the Catholic Church, they realize they are like casual fans of Jesus who want to become die-hard fans. The word *baptism* is derived from the Greek word *baptizein,* which literally means "to dip or immerse in water." A related word means "to dye," as in dying cloth. When an adult or infant is immersed in the water of Baptism, it is like he or she is dyed with the Holy Spirit and transformed. Anyone who has seen a die-hard fan painted with team colors can see that this person has been taken over by enthusiasm for it.

4. Use milk and chocolate syrup to help illustrate the image that we not only die with Christ but are dyed with Christ at Baptism. As you pour the chocolate syrup into the glass of milk, it sinks to the bottom. Illustrate that a person needs to stir it in order for it to become chocolate milk. Note that when we are dyed with Christ at Baptism, we can either push his identity to the bottom of the glass or we can welcome him and allow him to permeate our whole existence.

5. Conclude the activity by discussing this question with the young people:

- What can we do to stir up the presence of Christ within, to accept him more fully, to be more truly ourselves?

If you are using the student workbook, this would be an appropriate time to ask the young people to respond in writing to question 1 on page 12.

Resisting the Tempter with Jesus Today

Preparation

❑ Provide each student with a copy of *Breakthrough! The Bible for Young Catholics* or another Bible, a pen or pencil, and a sheet of paper.

1. Introduce the activity with thoughts along these lines:

- The devil's temptations to Jesus can be seen as tests to Jesus' true identity. Although the devil claims he is testing Jesus to see if he is God's Son, this temptation actually asks Jesus to compromise this identity.
- When we are tempted, we have a choice to affirm who we really are as children of God or to allow the temptation to shape our identity.

2. Arrange the students into groups of three. In their groups, have them read the three accounts of the temptations in Matthew 4:1–11, Mark 1:12–13, and Luke 4:1–13. Ask them to note the similarities and differences between the accounts. Ask these questions:

- What is the devil basically trying to do in tempting Jesus? Why?
- What is Jesus' basic answer to these temptations? Why?

3. Review the three ways the devil tempts Jesus. Note that though the devil might not tempt us in the same way, we struggle with some of the same issues that he tempted Jesus with.

- "If you are God's Son . . ." (Matthew 4:6) could be understood as a challenge to Jesus' identity. While we might have a natural desire to "prove ourselves," when do people tempt us by saying "prove it"? Do we tend to want to prove to ourselves and others that we are worthwhile?
- The devil tempts Jesus with power and wealth. Power and wealth are certainly temptations for many people.
- When the devil asks for the stone to be turned into bread and for Jesus to jump off the Temple, he asks him to do something "supernatural" or outside the regular forces of nature, something miraculous. Jesus used his miracles only to heal or help others. People can ask us to use our gifts selfishly rather than for others.

4. Discuss this question with the students:

- Is it easy to want to use our own gifts and talents just for ourselves rather than seeing them as gifts to be used in God's service?

5. Explore the ways Jesus resisted temptation. Ask the students to describe how he was able to do this. Aloud, reread Jesus' response to each temptation. Ask the group:

- Does Jesus suggest where we should turn when we feel tempted?

6. Ask the young people to fold a piece of paper into three columns. Give these directions:

- In the first column, write down five to seven talents and other good qualities you have.
- In the middle column, for each talent or quality, write down what it looks like if you use it just for yourself or to promote yourself.
- In the far right column, write down what the talent or quality looks like when you realize you are a son or daughter of God, a member of a community, and you use it for others.

7. To conclude the activity, converse about what makes it easy to use talents for others and what makes it difficult.

Variation

If you are short on time and are using the student workbook, ask the students to answer question 2 on page 12 and discuss their answers in place of steps 6 and 7 of this activity.

Chapter 3

Getting to Know Jesus and His Disciples

Preparing to Teach

Overview

Young adolescents are very concerned with their friends. Jesus also values friendship. In his friendship with the disciples, Jesus calls them to live like him and is himself a model of the servant leadership he preaches. Although some young adolescents are a poor example to their peers, many inspire and encourage their friends to virtue.

The length of Jesus' ministry is three short years. He knows his ministry must continue without him after his death and Resurrection. Jesus discerns and calls followers who are filled with the power of the Holy Spirit. He sends them out to preach, heal, and forgive sins. He begins by calling two fishermen, Peter and his brother Andrew. Aside from their unabashed desire to drop everything and follow Jesus, there is nothing remarkable about these men. They are not trained in theology, yet they are courageous enough to follow this Jesus whose radically different views on religious laws are concerning to some.

Jesus values friendship. He includes the Apostles in many important aspects of his life, the Last Supper being one of the most significant. It is at this meal that Jesus models the behavior he intends the Apostles to follow in their ministry. When Jesus removes his outer garment, ties a towel around his waist, and removes the men's sandals to wash their feet, he models the behavior he expects from the Apostles—that of servant. Jesus displays behaviors that represent a new covenant between God and human beings, one based on love and service.

People who love in a Christlike way, putting the welfare of others first, are living testimonies to the existence of Christ in our world. Jesus prays to the Father for the protection of his disciples; he knows the hardships they will face when ministering in his name. Today we the Church continue this mission, and our young adolescents are part of it!

This Chapter at a Glance

Getting to Know the Story of Jesus and His Disciples

- Chosen for Service

Getting to Know Jesus and His Disciples

- To Love and to Serve
- John, Chapter 17

Scripture Passages Related to Jesus and His Disciples

The passages listed in bold are readings the students will reference to complete the puzzle "Jesus and His Disciples" on page 13 of the *Student Activity Workbook for "Breakthrough! The Bible for Young Catholics": Getting to Know Jesus.*

- Matthew 4:18–22, **Mark 1:14–20,** Luke 5:1–11 (Jesus calls four fishermen.)*
- Matthew 9:9–13, **Mark 2:13–17,** Luke 5:27–32 (Jesus calls Matthew.)
- Matthew 8:18–22, Luke 9:57–62 (The would-be followers of Jesus)
- **Matthew 10:1–4,** Mark 3:13–19, Luke 6:12–16 (Jesus chooses the twelve Apostles.)*
- Matthew 10:5–15, Mark 6:7–13, Luke 9:1–6 (Jesus sends out the twelve disciples.)*
- Luke 8:1–3 (Women who accompanied Jesus)
- Luke 10:1–12 (Jesus sends out the seventy-two.)*
- Luke 14:25–33, Matthew 10:37,38 (The cost of being a disciple)
- **John 1:35–42** (The first disciples of Jesus)
- **John 1:43–51** (Jesus calls Philip and Nathanael.)
- John 13:1–20 (Jesus washes his disciples' feet.)*
- John 17:1–26 (Jesus prays for his disciples.)*

Asterisk (*) signifies key passages to cover.

Articles from *Breakthrough!* Related to Jesus and His Disciples

Break Through!

- The Twelve (Matthew 10:1–4)
- Called and Sent (Mark 3:13–19)

- Peter the Rock (Matthew 16:13–20)
- What? No Cell Phone? (Mark 6:6–13)
- Jesus: A Friend and Teacher to All (Luke 8:1–3)
- Shame on You (Luke 9:23–27)
- Two by Two (Luke 10:1–12)
- Mary as the First Disciple (John 2:1–12)

Jesus, His Disciples, and Young Adolescents Today

- Jesus has twelve special friends, the Apostles. Young adolescents also have special relationships with friends.
- The Apostles are a diverse group of men. Adolescents embrace friends of different cultural, economic, social, and religious backgrounds.
- Jesus is a loyal friend. Students value loyalty in their friendships.
- Jesus forgives Peter when Peter denies knowing Jesus. Young adolescents have the experience of being forgiven by friends, and by God through the sacrament of Penance and Reconciliation.
- Jesus shares his intimate thoughts and emotions with the Apostles. Young people share their intimate thoughts and emotions with their best friends.
- Jesus relies on his closest disciples to be with him during difficult times in his life. Students also rely on friends to help them through difficult times.
- Jesus prays for his disciples. Young adolescents often pray for friends in need or for their families.

Getting to Know the Story of Jesus and His Disciples

Note: If you are using the student workbook, the puzzle "Jesus and His Disciples" on page 13 is a good way to familiarize the young people with several of these biblical stories. See appendix 2 of this manual for the solution to the puzzle.

Chosen for Service

In this activity the students create a plan to attract others to participate in an event for a specific social justice issue or charity.

Preparation

- [ ] Provide copies of *Breakthrough! The Bible for Young Catholics* or another Bible, one for each young person.

1. Before gathering for this activity, have the students choose a particular social justice or charitable organization to research. Have them collect information about it from the Internet, and ask them to note whether the organization has a specific way of fund-raising (a bike-a-thon, a walk-a-thon, etc.).

2. Distribute the bibles and ask the students to follow along as you read Luke 5:1–11,27–32 and Luke 6:12–16 aloud. Discuss these readings with the young people. Ask them to consider why Jesus chose the twelve men to be trained as Apostles. Explain that Jesus wanted them to carry on his ministry when he would no longer be with them.

3. Suggest the following idea to the group:

- Suppose you wanted to actively carry on Jesus' ministry by becoming involved in a social justice effort or charity outreach. How would you go about doing this?

4. Ask the students to write a letter to the school at large. (This will be an exercise rather than a real campaign.) Give these instructions:

- The letter should describe who you are and why you choose to assist this social justice organization or charity with its unique cause.

- In the body of your letter, include comments that will encourage others to join with you in supporting this cause.

(Although this letter is simply a tool to explore the Gospel message of discipleship, it will help each student become aware of his or her ability to be part of Jesus' ministry as a disciple.)

5. Conclude the activity by having the students share their letters with fellow classmates. You may want to have the students vote on one social justice organization or charity as an opportunity to do a schoolwide or parishwide fund-raiser. Help the young people recognize the parallel between Jesus' way of gathering people to assist him in his ministry and what the students themselves could do with others to better the world.

Getting to Know Jesus and His Disciples

To Love and to Serve

In this activity students reflect on Jesus' interactions with the disciples at the Last Supper and then design "acts of service" coupon books for their families.

Preparation

- ❑ Provide copies of *Breakthrough! The Bible for Young Catholics* or another Bible, one for each young person.
- ❑ Provide the class with drawing paper, coloring implements, and one or more staplers.

1. Distribute the bibles and have students read the story of Jesus' washing his disciples' feet in John 13:1–20. Then read the story out loud slowly, focusing on the contradictions Jesus introduces to the Apostles.

2. Give background information as to what was typically done in Jesus' day when guests entered a house. Stress that foot washing was usually reserved for the lowest slave. Jesus' behavior was shocking to the Apostles!

Have the students share their thoughts in response to these questions:

- ❍ Do you understand why Peter first told Jesus he could not wash his feet?
- ❍ Can you think of a situation today that would be an example of such a switch in power? (Invite the students to share a similar story. An example might be the governor's cleaning their shoes after they stepped in a dog's mess.)
- ❍ If we today do not let Jesus serve us as he did the Apostles, are we in danger of no longer being his disciples?
- ❍ Do you understand why Peter wants a more complete bath after learning how key this cleansing is to being Jesus' disciple?
- ❍ What are some adjectives that could describe the love Jesus is showing his disciples?
- ❍ What are the reasons behind Jesus' act of service?

Note that the young people can answer the last two questions in writing using question 1 on page 14 of the student workbook.

3. Ask a student to reread John 13:12–17. Have another student paraphrase the passage. Then ask all the young people to brainstorm ways they could model Jesus' actions in their families. (Examples might be cleaning one's room, walking the dog, washing the dishes, taking out the garbage, etc.) Challenge the students to come up with service ideas that go beyond what is generally expected of them.

4. Tell the young people they will now create a coupon book that will entitle their family to five acts of service free of charge. The students can use their creativity in making the coupons, but they could also just use a single 8½-x-11-inch sheet of paper to make several coupons. Distribute the art materials, and explain that the students should make a cover and a back page for their coupon book.

5. Conclude the activity by having the young people report back about the success of their coupon books at home.

John, Chapter 17

In this activity the young people write their own prayers for loved ones based on Jesus' prayer for his disciples.

Preparation

- ❑ Provide copies of *Breakthrough! The Bible for Young Catholics* or another Bible, one for each young person.
- ❑ Make copies of handout 3-A, "John, Chapter 17: Praying for Others," one for each student.

1. Explain to the students that the prayer in John, chapter 17 is one of intercession, talking to God on behalf of others.

2. Allow the students time to read the prayer quietly to themselves. Then offer the following insight about the prayer:

- ❍ Jesus is concerned with the events the disciples will encounter in the near future. Life will be filled with challenges, so he asks God the Father to protect the disciples from the hostile world. Before Jesus prays for them, he gives glory to God the Father.

3. Allow the students some time to reflect on any current or future concerns they may have about family or friends and to jot those concerns down privately. If you are using the student workbook, students may instead write down a few things they would like help with as a response to question 2 on page 14.

4. Distribute copies of handout 3-A, "John, Chapter 17: Praying for Others," to the young people. Using the model provided on the handout, have the young people write their own intercessory prayers.

John, Chapter 17: Praying for Others

Brainstorm personal family issues that are of concern to you as well as any issues that may be troubling your friends. Using the outline below as a guide, write a personal intercessory prayer in the blank space.

1. In the first paragraph, give glory to God.

2. In the second paragraph, list the intercessions you have brainstormed.

3. In the third paragraph, pray for unity.

4. In the final paragraph, describe what you intend to do to make God known to others.

Chapter 4
Getting to Know Jesus in Prayer

Preparing to Teach

Overview

The majority of young adolescents pray, but they may be only beginning to understand what it means to be a person of prayer like Jesus is. Your young adolescents may or may not have support for spiritual growth at home. A regular pattern of seeking solitude for prayer may seem foreign to some young people who are very interested in communicating with their friends, whether that be by phone, by text message, or in person. They may need some help understanding the value of solitude, whether that be in nature, in the school chapel, or in their bedroom.

Jesus learns to pray in a devout family that actively participates in the Jewish spiritual life. As a young adolescent, Jesus experiences an intensification of his spiritual life when, at the age of twelve, he is found in the Temple.

Jesus' prayer springs from this passionate desire to be with God. As much as Jesus is "God with us," he very much lives his life "with God." Throughout his ministry, Jesus has a steady, regular pattern of rising early (or staying up all night) to pray in out-of-the-way places and on hillsides. We see Jesus praying in the midst of ordinary life events as well as during important ones. His relationship with the Father grows through the joys and struggles of life.

Jesus' followers cannot help but notice this important part of his daily life and eventually inquire about learning how to pray like him (see Matt. 6:7–15). Why? They want to grow in their relationship with God as Jesus does. There is something about the praying Jesus that fascinates and draws his followers to learn more.

Young adolescents certainly have ordinary and extraordinary events in their lives and encounter challenges and struggles. Jesus' prayer life may not have made difficulties go away, but the students should be able to see that Jesus approaches difficulties very differently because of his close relationship with his Father. Learning to pray means patterning our prayer lives after Jesus as well as asking for the grace to share his desire to be with God.

This Chapter at a Glance

Getting to Know the Story of Jesus in Prayer

- Learning to Pray from the Expert

Getting to Know Jesus in Prayer

- "Lord, Teach Us to Pray"

Scripture Passages Related to Jesus in Prayer

The passages listed in bold are readings the students will reference to complete the puzzle "Jesus in Prayer" on page 15 of the *Student Activity Workbook for "Breakthrough! The Bible for Young Catholics": Getting to Know Jesus.*

- **Matthew 6:5–6** (Teaching about prayer)*
- **Matthew 6:7–15,** Luke 11:1–4 (Our Father)*
- Matthew 7:7–12, **Luke 11:5–13** (Ask, seek, knock)*
- **Mark 1:35–39** (Jesus preaches in Galilee.)
- **Luke 5:15–16** (Jesus prays in lonely places.)
- **Luke 6:12–16** (Jesus chooses the twelve Apostles.)
- Mark 9:2–9, **Matthew 17:1–13,** Luke 9:28–36 (The Transfiguration)
- **Matthew 11:25–27**, Luke 10:21–23 (Jesus prays in thanks.)
- **Luke 18:1–8** (The parable of the widow and the judge)*
- **Luke 18:9–13** (The parable of the Pharisee and the tax collector)*

Asterisk (*) signifies key passages to cover.

Articles from *Breakthrough!* Related to Jesus in Prayer

- Shine Bright (Matthew 5:13–16)
- No Show-Offs (Matthew 6:5–7)
- Obstacles to Prayer (Matthew 26:36–46)
- I Messed Up Again, Jesus (Mark 14:32–72)
- Turn Down the Noise (Luke 4:42–43)
- The Our Father: Another Version (Luke 11:1–4)
- Prayers of Petition (Luke 11:9–13)
- Common Cents (Luke 20:19–26)

Jesus in Prayer and Young Adolescents Today

- Jesus' prayer life is influenced by his family experience of faith. Young adolescents also come from backgrounds that affect the way they think about prayer and their prayer practices. For some, prayer has been nurtured at home; for others, it has been absent; and yet for others, it has been discouraged.

- Jesus often goes to an outdoor setting to pray. Young people are also drawn to nature for reflection.
- Jesus teaches the Lord's Prayer as a model for prayer. Though the young people probably know how to *say* the Lord's Prayer, they might need to be encouraged to *pray* it as prayer of praise, repentance, and petition.
- For Jesus, prayer is taking time to be with God in a consistent way through easy times and hard times. Young people can be invited to grow in relationship with God like Jesus so that they bring all their concerns to God as a regular part of their lives.

Getting to Know the Story of Jesus in Prayer

Learning to Pray from the Expert

In this activity students become familiar with Scripture passages in which Jesus prays and teaches or tells stories about prayer. The young people also summarize some of the key qualities that Jesus emphasizes.

Preparation

- ❑ Provide copies of *Breakthrough! The Bible for Young Catholics* or another Bible, one for each young person.
- ❑ Make copies of handout 4–A, "Jesus, the Expert on Prayer," one for each student.

1. Distribute the bibles and the copies of handout 4–A, "Jesus, the Expert on Prayer." Have the young people complete the handout either individually or in small groups.

2. Go over the handout with the students, asking for input about the most important aspects of Jesus' teaching in a particular passage. As a whole class, try to find a word that summarizes even further what Jesus is asking from us in each Scripture passage. For example, Matthew 6:5–6 could be summarized by saying, "Pray in your room rather than in places that are public," or it might be captured by the word *humility.* Have the students record their responses on the handout.

Consider using this list that characterizes prayer when you or the young people prepare a type of prayer.

If the young people have the student workbook, this would be a good time to assign question 1 on page 16 and to discuss the students' reflections.

Students will also be well prepared to complete the puzzle "Jesus in Prayer" on page 15 of the workbook. The puzzle would be a good review of this material. See appendix 2 of this manual for the solution to the puzzle.

Getting to Know Jesus in Prayer

"Lord, Teach Us to Pray"

In this activity the young people examine the different parts of the Lord's Prayer and then write the prayer in their own words.

If the young people have the student workbook and you are short on time, you may want to have them work on question 2 on page 16 of the workbook, which summarizes the main points of this activity.

Preparation

- ❑ Provide each student with a copy of *Breakthrough! The Bible for Young Catholics* or another Bible and a pen or pencil.
- ❑ Make copies of handout 4–B, "Reflecting on the Lord's Prayer," one for each young person.

1. Introduce the activity by saying that Jesus describes some of the key attributes of prayer and shows the results of a rich prayerful life.

2. Distribute the bibles and have the young people follow along as you read Matthew 6:7–15 aloud. Ask them why this prayer is so important.

3. Distribute handout 4–B, "Reflecting on the Lord's Prayer," to the young people. Postpone reading the directions for now. Help the students recognize significant parts of the Lord's Prayer by asking the following questions:

- Where do we ask for mercy?
- Where do we praise God?
- Where do we petition God for things we need?
- Should these three elements be part of our regular prayer, whether we are saying the Lord's Prayer or not?

4. Read the directions on the handout with the students. Provide some quiet time for the young people to work on the handout individually.

5. Invite some of the students to share what they wrote down on the handout. Mention that "translating" the Lord's Prayer can be a type of prayer—one that attempts to understand the words and phrases more deeply. Provide the students with these other ideas about the Lord's Prayer. Consider using the ideas with the students during your prayer sessions with them.

- Say the Lord's Prayer as slowly as you can. Take a phrase of it and repeat it to yourself ten times before moving on to the next phrase.
- Pray only one section of the Lord's Prayer per day. Repeat it throughout the day and consider what it means. The next day, add another section to it. Repeat the process until you have completed the prayer.

Jesus, the Expert on Prayer

Read through the Scripture passages below and write a summary statement or two about what Jesus tells us about prayer.

Matthew 6:5–6

Matthew 6:7–15

Matthew 11:25–27

Matthew 11:28–30

Mark 1:35–39

Luke 5:15–16

Luke 6:12–16

Luke 11:5–13

Luke 18:1–8

Luke 18:9–14

Reflecting on the Lord's Prayer

Next to each phrase from the Lord's Prayer, write another version of the phrase, using more current language or simply putting the words in a different way.

Our Father,

who art in heaven,

hallowed be thy name;

thy kingdom come;

thy will be done

on earth

as it is in heaven.

Give us this day

our daily bread;

and forgive us our trespasses

as we forgive

those who trespass against us;

and lead us

not into temptation,

but deliver us

from evil.

Amen.

(This prayer is adapted from the *Sacramentary,* English translation prepared by the International Commission on English in the Liturgy [New York: Catholic Book Publishing Company, 1985], page 561. Illustrations and arrangement copyright © 1985–1974 by Catholic Book Publishing Company, New York.)

Chapter 5

Getting to Know Gospel Images of Jesus

Preparing to Teach

Overview

Young adolescents are preoccupied with personal revelation. "Should I tell her what I really feel?" "What will people think of me if I post these poems and pictures of myself online?" "What do my clothes say about me?" "Did I make a fool of myself at that assembly?" In the Gospels Jesus teaches us who he is through word and action. Jesus not only lovingly reveals who he is but also models what it means to share oneself with others.

The Gospel writers provide us with different portrayals of Jesus. John begins his Gospel with a description of Christ, the Eternal Word of God. This chapter focuses on images of Jesus in the Gospel of John. God intensely desires to communicate with us. As we read further in John's Gospel, we learn that the Word becomes flesh in Jesus. It is through this incarnation that we come to know God intimately, because to know Jesus is to know God. The person and teachings of Jesus allow us to experience God more fully. We experience a God who is actively involved with every aspect of our human lives.

Jesus uses many beautiful images in John's Gospel, mainly to let his followers know who he is. If we reflect on the biblical relationship between the shepherd and the sheep, we come to understand the level of care and concern Jesus is expressing. One of the most startling truths of faith Jesus gives us is that of resurrection. Jesus states to Martha in John 11:25: "I am the resurrection and the life. Those who believe in me will live, even though they die." In John, chapter 15, Jesus gives his disciples the encouragement they need to face the difficult task of carrying on his work. Through the images of the grapevine and the branches, he promises that God nurtures and supports anyone who stays close to Jesus.

When Jesus reveals himself, he brings love, hope, and the knowledge of God that leads to faith. When we share something about ourselves, do we always do so in love? Do our actions sustain other people's faith in God? When we ask others to tell us about themselves, do we do this in a sense of hope? Using Jesus' self-revelation is a good guide for young adolescents as they decide what is appropriate to share in their relationships with others.

This Chapter at a Glance

Getting to Know the Story with Gospel Images of Jesus

- Jesus the Resurrection and the Life

Getting to Know Jesus Through Gospel Images

- Jesus the Good Shepherd
- Jesus the Real Vine

Scripture Passages Related to Gospel Images of Jesus

The following Scripture passages are readings the students will study to complete the puzzle "Gospel Images of Jesus" on page 17 of the *Student Activity Workbook for "Breakthrough! The Bible for Young Catholics": Getting to Know Jesus.*

- **John 1:1–18** (The Word of life)*
- **John 3:1–21** (Jesus and Nicodemus)*
- John 4:1–42 (Jesus and the Samaritan woman)
- John 5:19–29 (The authority of the Son)
- John 5:30–47 (Witnesses to Jesus)
- **John 6:25–59** (Jesus the bread of life)*
- John 7:37–39 (Streams of life-giving water)*
- **John 8:12–20** (Jesus the light of the world)*
- **John 10:1–21** (Jesus the Good Shepherd)*
- **John 11:17–27** (Jesus the Resurrection and the life)*
- John 14:1–14 (Jesus the way to the Father)*
- **John 15:1–17** (Jesus the real vine)*

Asterisk (*) signifies key passages to cover.

Articles from *Breakthrough!* Related to Gospel Images of Jesus

Break Through!

- John 3:16 (John 3:16)
- Filling Up (John 7:37–39)
- The "I Am" Sayings (John 8:12)
- Jesus the Firefighter? (John 10:7–21)

Gospel Images of Jesus and Young Adolescents Today

- Jesus is the Word incarnate. Young adolescents can identify with the human nature of Jesus.
- Jesus is the living water who will quench all who thirst. Young adolescents have emotional, physical, and spiritual thirsts.
- Jesus is the Good Shepherd. A shepherd takes care of his sheep. Many young people have either experienced human models of Jesus' shepherding or yearn for it. Oftentimes young people of this age are good at shepherding younger children.
- Jesus teaches that he is the Resurrection and the life. When facing end-of-life issues concerning family and friends, students can find hope in the Christian teaching about death and resurrection.

Getting to Know the Story with Gospel Images of Christ

Jesus the Resurrection and the Life

In this activity the students explore images of Jesus and use these references to create sympathy cards.

If you do not have time to complete the artwork, consider having the young people choose passages they would find helpful at a difficult time for them. If the young people have the workbook, they can do this by answering question 2 on page 18.

Preparation

- ❑ Provide each young person with a copy of *Breakthrough! The Bible for Young Catholics* or another Bible, a pen or pencil, a sheet of paper, and crayons or markers.

1. Introduce this activity by talking about the experience of death in a family. Have the students suggest the types of things families do to cope with grief or to honor a loved one who has died. Then ask them to talk about things friends do to support each other during grief. (If any young person would like to share something from his or her personal experience of a death, allow him or her to do so.)

2. Distribute the bibles. Write the following Scripture citations on the board and ask the students to take turns reading the passages aloud to the class. Note that these are readings that could be consoling to people when they have lost a loved one.

- **John 1:1–18** (The Word of life)
- **John 6:25–59** (Jesus the bread of life)
- **John 7:37–39** (Streams of life-giving water)
- **John 8:12–20** (Jesus the light of the world)
- **John 11:17–27** (Jesus the Resurrection and the life)
- **John 14:1–14** (Jesus the way to the Father)

3. Distribute the paper, crayons or markers, and pens or pencils to the students. Ask each of them to create a sample sympathy card using words from the passages they just read. (Explain that the cards will not be sent.) Suggest that the young people can remind a person that their loved one is with Jesus or help that person cope with the loss itself. On the back of their cards, have the young people write a paragraph that explains why they chose the particular passage over the others. Discuss their choices and why certain passages communicate hope.

Note: After completing this activity, the students will be well prepared to complete the puzzle "Gospel Images of Jesus" on page 17 of the student workbook. See appendix 2 of this manual for the solution to the puzzle.

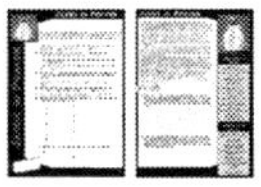

Getting to Know Jesus Through Gospel Images

Jesus the Good Shepherd

In this activity the students identify Jesus as the Good Shepherd who cares for his flock.

Preparation

- ❑ Provide each student with a copy of *Breakthrough! The Bible for Young Catholics* or another Bible and a pen or pencil.
- ❑ Make copies of handout 5-A, "Jesus the Good Shepherd," one for each young person.

1. Distribute the bibles and then begin the activity by inviting the students to read John 10:7–21, the story of Jesus the Good Shepherd.

2. Provide the students with the following background information about shepherds and their sheep in biblical times:

- ❍ In Israel most sheep were used for their wool and therefore were not slaughtered. The shepherd had a close relationship with his sheep. They responded to his distinct voice and would follow when called. Between the sheep and the shepherd, there existed a relationship based on trust and a sense of security.

Throughout the Bible there are references to Jesus as shepherd and his people as his flock.

3. Distribute copies of handout 5-A, "Jesus the Good Shepherd," to the students and allow time for them to complete it.

4. Conclude the activity by having the students share their findings with the class. Discuss whether the students were surprised at how often the analogy of Jesus as shepherd and the people as his flock is used in the Scriptures to describe the relationship of God with his people. Ask a student to read "Jesus the Firefighter?" (John 10:7-21) from *Breakthrough! The Bible for Young Catholics.* What other analogies might we use today to describe this shepherd-sheep relationship?

If the young people are using the workbook, have them complete question 1 on page 18 in writing prior to discussing it as a class.

Jesus the Real Vine

In this activity the students take the message about Jesus in the Book of John as the real vine and make it personal and relevant to their own lives.

Preparation

- ❑ Provide each student with a copy of *Breakthrough! The Bible for Young Catholics* or another Bible, a sheet of paper, and a pen or pencil.

1. Distribute the bibles, paper, and pens or pencils. Read John 15:1-17 aloud, asking the students to follow along in their bibles. Discuss with the young people the relationship Jesus is presenting in this passage. Also talk about the principle behind pruning a plant back so it actually increases its yield.

2. Have students divide their sheets of paper into three columns. Give them these instructions:

- In the first column, list personality traits you have that need pruning, such as a tendency to cheat, lie, or be lazy.
- In the second column, list ways you can avoid these traits that make it hard to grow spiritually. An example might be studying for exams to avoid the temptation to cheat.
- In the third column, list the "fruits," or ways you can use your gifts to serve God.

Conclude this activity by reminding the students that Jesus gives us simple advice about transforming our shortcomings from the first column into the fruits of the third: “A branch cannot bear fruit by itself; it can do so only if it remains in the vine. In the same way you cannot bear fruit unless you remain in me” (John 15:4).

Jesus the Good Shepherd

Locate the following Scripture passages in the Bible. Write each verse on the lines provided.

Psalm 23:1____

Psalm 80:1____

Isaiah 40:11______________________________________

Ezekiel 34:1______________________________________

Psalm 77:20______________________________________

Psalm 95:7____

Mark 14:27____

1 Peter 2:25______________________________________

Psalm 79:13______________________________________

Psalm 100:3______________________________________

Matthew 18:12____________________________________

Luke 12:32____

Hebrews 13:20____________________________________

(This list is adapted from the God's Word for the Biblically Inept series, *Life of Christ*, volume 2, by Robert C. Girard and Larry Richards [Lancaster, PA: Starburst Publications, 2000], page 79. Copyright © 2000 by Starburst Publications.)

What are five adjectives that describe the relationship between God and his people?

Chapter 6

Getting to Know Jesus the Teacher

Preparing to Teach

Overview

Jesus is a model teacher for all of us. Jesus' teachings all pertained to the Kingdom of God, so that by learning about Jesus the teacher, we learn more about the Reign of heaven he shows us.

A difficulty in discussing Jesus' teachings about the Kingdom of God is the image of medieval castles and royalty that the word *kingdom* tends to evoke in people's minds. Even the use of a parallel term, such as *Reign of God,* elicits images of grand patrons governing a territory with benign intent yet far removed from the life of the inhabitants. Nothing could be further from the truth of the Kingdom of God.

For Jesus the Kingdom of God occurs when people live in peace, righteousness, and joy in the Holy Spirit. The Reign of God is mysteriously present already, but ultimately it transforms all things to God's purpose. This inherent tension between the Reign of God being both *present* and *still to come* is difficult to explain.

Because of Jesus' Passion, death, and Resurrection, we know that God acts in the world and brings God's will about through the lives of believers everywhere, despite the presence of suffering and sin. The Kingdom of God seems invisible in the worldly sense, but God is faithful; with the gift of faith, we, as Kingdom of God disciples, can see people living the values of Jesus today and can confidently pray, "Your kingdom come, your will be done, on earth as it is heaven."

This Chapter at a Glance

Getting to Know the Story of Jesus the Teacher

- *Kingdom of God Bingo*

Getting to Know Jesus the Teacher

- "Your Kingdom Come"

Scripture Passages Related to Jesus the Teacher

The passages listed in bold are readings the students will reference to complete the puzzle "Jesus the Teacher" on page 19 of the *Student Activity Workbook for "Breakthrough! The Bible for Young Catholics": Getting to Know Jesus.*

- **Matthew 5:3–12,** Luke 6:20–23 (True happiness)
- **Matthew 6:25–33;** Luke 12:22–31, 16:13 (God and possessions)*
- **Matthew 13:44–46** (The parable of the hidden treasure, the parable of the pearl)*
- Matthew 20:1–16 (The workers in the vineyard)
- Matthew 25:14–30, **Luke 19:11–27** (The parable of the gold coins)*
- **Matthew 25:31–46** (The Final Judgment)*
- Matthew 19:22–26, **Mark 10:23–27,** Luke 18:24–27 (Riches and the Kingdom)
- Matthew 22:34–40, Mark 12:28–34, Luke 10:25–28 (The great commandment)*
- **Luke 17:20–21** ("The Kingdom of God is within you.")
- **John 3:5–7** (Being born of the Spirit)
- John 14:1–14 (Jesus the way to the Father)
- Matthew 27:1,2,11–14; Mark 15:1–15; Luke 23:1–5; **John 18:28–38** (The Kingdom is not of this world.)

Asterisk (*) signifies key passages to cover

Break Through!

Articles from *Breakthrough!* Related to Jesus the Teacher

- Jesus' Most Famous Sermon (Matthew, chapters 5–7)
- The God Box (Matthew, chapter 13)
- Truly Free (Matthew, chapter 19)
- Defending Poor People (Matthew 21:1–17)
- Seeing Christ, Being Christ (Matthew 25:31–46)
- Story Time! (Mark, chapter 4)
- The Challenge (Mark 10:17–31)
- Laws of Love (Mark 12:28–34)
- Old News (Luke 5:36–39)
- Jesus: A Friend and Teacher to All (Luke 8:1–3)
- You Better Watch Out (Luke 21:7–19)
- Being Good Seeds (John 12:22–26)

Jesus the Teacher and Young Adolescents Today

- Jesus' teachings about the Kingdom of God are challenging but also attractive to young people.
- Jesus shares parables about the Kingdom of God that may appear simple but are also complex. The parables, though apparently easy to decode, often present some unexpected ideas that need to be explained to young adolescents.
- Just as Jesus experienced the presence of both God and sin in the world, young people notice the tension between the fullness of the Kingdom of God in Jesus and its incompleteness in our world. Just as Jesus lived in this tension with hope, young people can believe that despite the hidden nature of the Kingdom of God at times, it is nonetheless undeniably real and ultimately more enduring than this world.
- Jesus is the model for teachers. Though young people should be encouraged to see good teachers in their midst, they should also remember that they themselves are teachers of the Good News through their words and actions, especially in relation to younger children.

Getting to Know the Story of Jesus the Teacher

Kingdom of God Bingo

Preparation

- ❑ Provide copies of *Breakthrough! The Bible for Young Catholics* or another Bible, one for each student.
- ❑ Make enough copies of the bingo cards on resource 6-A, "*Kingdom of God Bingo* Cards," for each small group of four to have four different cards.
- ❑ Make enough copies of the readings from resource 6-B, "Kingdom of God Readings," for each small group of four to have one.
- ❑ Provide scissors for the young people to cut up the reading sections and enough markers or pennies for all the bingo cards being used in the session.

1. Introduce the activity with thoughts along these lines:

   - ❍ Jesus is the role model for every teacher. He not only taught lovingly but imparted a message necessary for the salvation of all those who heard him. Very importantly, he "walked his talk," meaning he actually lived the content of his message. Much of Jesus' teaching centered around the Kingdom of God that occurs when people live in peace, righteousness, and joy in the Holy Spirit.

We will be reviewing some of Jesus' important teachings about the Kingdom of God through a bingo game.

2. Divide the class into groups of four and distribute a set of four different *Kingdom of God Bingo* cards to each small group. Give each group a scissors and a copy of resource-B, "Kingdom of God Readings," to cut up for their game as well as a sufficient number of markers or coins for their playing cards. Distribute a Bible to each student. (Note that if a translation other than the *Good News Translation,* Catholic Version, is used, there may be differences in wording between the biblical text and the text on the bingo cards.)

3. Give these instructions to the groups:

- Assign one student in your group to randomly select a reading slip and read the Scripture passage cited there.
- Each one of you should look up the citation. As you begin to read the Scripture passage, compare it with the excerpt on your *Kingdom of God Bingo* card. Some of your cards will have part of this Scripture passage in one of the squares. If your card has part of this reading, put a marker on that square.
- Continue playing in this way. When you have three matched Scriptures in a row on your card, shout "Kingdom of God!"
- Do not stop playing when you have a column or row. The real "winner" is the group that reads all the Scriptures well and finishes first.

Getting to Know Jesus the Teacher

"Your Kingdom Come"

Preparation

- ☐ Provide copies of *Breakthrough! The Bible for Young Catholics* or another Bible, one for each student.
- ☐ Make copies of handout 6-A, "'It's All About God' Versus 'It's All About Me,'" one for each young person.
- ☐ Provide a pen or pencil for each student.

1. Introduce this activity by sharing the following thoughts in your own words:

- You have likely seen the shirts and other items that say, "It's all about me!" Though these shirts are made for fun, they do have a message that is lived out by people in our culture and perhaps by every person at some time in their lives.

- Jesus taught about the Kingdom of God. For Jesus the Kingdom of God occurs when people live in peace, righteousness, and joy in the Holy Spirit. Then God's Spirit reigns over people's hearts, minds, and actions. When the Kingdom of God reigns, it is "all about God."

- When it is "all about God," it does not mean the individual person disappears or is not important. It means that people regularly discern what God wants them to do and then they do it. The Kingdom of God says that if you do what God wants, you will be deeply happy. We also receive messages that say that if you always do what you want, you will be deeply happy.

2. Ask the group to answer these questions by conversing in pairs or triads. Discuss them as a large group to try and assign some characteristics to each viewpoint.

- These messages conflict. Can you think of any characters on TV, sports figures, or other famous people who are living out "It's all about God" the best they can? Can you think of people who live out "It's all about me"? What are the characteristics of each group?

3. Share the following thoughts with the students:

- If we want to know what it means to perfectly live out "It's all about God," we can look to Jesus. Notice that for him, being "all about God" did not mean that he never thought of himself or never took care of himself; he spent time with his friends, he took time to pray alone, and so on.

- The trouble lies in the "all" of each phrase. If anyone is ever "all" about themselves, they are living contrary to the Gospel and Jesus' message of the Kingdom of God. Following Jesus' teachings about the Kingdom of God enables us to live in harmony and love one another like God wants us to. Though we can never do this perfectly, we need to choose daily to "be about God" or to "be about ourselves."

4. Distribute the bibles, the copies of handout 6–A, "'It's All About God' Versus 'It's All About Me,'" and the pens or pencils. Read over the handout directions with the students and provide quiet time for them to complete the activity.

5. Ask the students to share what they have written as well as any observations they made while completing the handout. Ask:

- Do you hear messages from either the "It's All About God" or the "It's All About Me" columns in the culture around you?

Note: If the young people are using the student workbook, they can first answer in writing question 1 on page 20. The second reflection question on that page invites them to apply advertising techniques to messages about the Kingdom of God.

Kingdom of God Bingo Cards

Kingdom of God Bingo: Card A		
"Happy are those who know they are spiritually poor. . . ."	". . . the Kingdom of heaven belongs to them!"	". . . be concerned about everything else with the Kingdom of God and with what he requires of you, and he will provide."
". . . only those who do what my Father in heaven wants them to do."	". . . turn away from your sins and believe the Good News!"	". . . to enter the Kingdom of God."
"You are not far from the Kingdom of God."	"When the grain is ripe, the man starts cutting it with his sickle. . . ."	"A man takes a mustard seed, the smallest seed in the world and plants it. . . ."

(These Scripture quotations are from the *Good News Bible* © 1994 published by the Bible Societies/HarperCollins Publishers Ltd., *UK Good News Bible* © American Bible Society 1966, 1971, 1976, 1992. Used with permission.)

Kingdom of God Bingo: Card B		
". . . and then to gather in the wheat and put it into my barn."	". . . he goes and sells everything he has, and buys that pearl."	"So those who are last will be first, and those who are first will be last."
"For to every person who has something, even more will be given. . . ."	"Whenever you did this for one of the least important of these followers of mine, you did it for me!"	". . . the Kingdom of God is within you."
"Go out to the country roads and lanes and make people come in. . . ."	"Happy are those who know they are spiritually poor. . . ."	". . . the Kingdom of heaven belongs to them."

(These Scripture quotations are from the *Good News Bible* © 1994 published by the Bible Societies/HarperCollins Publishers Ltd., *UK Good News Bible* © American Bible Society 1966, 1971, 1976, 1992. Used with permission.)

Kingdom of God Bingo: Card C		
". . . be concerned about everything else with the Kingdom of God and with what he requires of you, and he will provide."	". . . only those who do what my Father in heaven wants them to do."	"Turn away from your sins and believe the Good News!"
"You are not far from the Kingdom of God."	". . . to enter the Kingdom of God."	"When the grain is ripe, the man starts cutting it with his sickle. . . ."
"A man takes a mustard seed, the smallest seed in the world and plants it. . . ."	". . . and then to gather in the wheat and put it into my barn."	". . . he goes and sells everything he has and buys that pearl."

Kingdom of God Bingo: Card D		
"So those who are last will be first, and those who are first will be last."	"For to every person who has something, even more will be given. . . ."	"Whenever you did this for one of the least important of these followers of mine, you did it for me!"
"Go out to the country roads and lanes and make people come in. . . ."	". . . the Kingdom of God is within you."	"Happy are those who know they are spiritually poor. . . ."
". . . the Kingdom of heaven belongs to them."	". . . be concerned about everything else with the Kingdom of God and with what he requires of you, and he will provide."	". . . only those who do what my Father in heaven wants them to do."

(These Scripture quotations are from the *Good News Bible* © 1994 published by the Bible Societies/HarperCollins Publishers Ltd., *UK Good News Bible* © American Bible Society 1966, 1971, 1976, 1992. Used with permission.)

Kingdom of God Readings

Matthew 5:3	Matthew 25:31-46
Matthew 5:10	Mark 1:14–15
Matthew 6:31–33	Mark 4:26–29
Matthew 7:21	Mark 4:30–32
Matthew 13:24–30	Mark 10:23–27
Matthew 13:44–46	Mark 12:28–34
Matthew 20:1–16	Luke 14:15–23
Matthew 25:14–30	Luke 17:20-21

"It's All About God" Versus "It's All About Me"

Look up the Kingdom of God Scripture passage(s) and summarize the main idea in the story or saying in the "It's All About God" column. Under the other column for that same passage, write how someone writing from an "It's All About Me" point of view would state the main point. See the first example.

Scripture Passage	It's All About God	It's All About Me
Matthew 5:3. "Happy are those who know they are spiritually poor; / the Kingdom of heaven belongs to them!"		Happy are those who are materially rich, for everything they want belongs to them.
Matthew 5:10. "Happy are those who are persecuted / because they do what God requires; / the Kingdom of heaven belongs to them!"		
Matthew 6:34. "Do not worry about tomorrow. . . ."		
Matthew 7:21. "Not everyone who calls me 'Lord, Lord' will enter the Kingdom of heaven. . . ."		
Matthew 13:24–30. The Parable of the Weeds		
Matthew 13:44–46. The Parable of the Hidden Treasure, The Parable of the Pearl		
Matthew 20:1–16. The Workers in the Vineyard		
Matthew 25:14–30. The Parable of the Three Servants		
Matthew 25:31–46. The Final Judgment		
Mark 1:15. "Turn away from your sins and believe the Good News."		
Mark 4:26–29. The Parable of the Growing Seed		
Mark 4:30–32. The Parable of the Mustard Seed		
Mark 10:23. "How hard it will be for rich people to enter the Kingdom of God!"		
Mark 12:28–34. The Great Commandment		
Luke 14:15–23. The Parable of the Great Feast		
Luke 17:20–21. "The Kingdom of God is within you."		

Chapter 7

Getting to Know Jesus the Healer

Preparing to Teach

Overview

Whether or not they give their longing this name, young adolescents long for healing in their lives. Unfortunately, they do not always think or know to go to Jesus for this healing. Whether or not they need additional professional attention for this healing, they need to remember that Jesus walks with everyone who is suffering and is a healing presence in ways they cannot imagine.

During the course of his ministry, Jesus performs many miracles. When we take a closer look at some of the physical healings he performs, we are able to see beyond the obvious details in the stories. In the Healing a Paralytic story, for example, several men carry their paralyzed friend to Jesus to be healed. Jesus sees their faith and responds to the paralyzed man by saying, "My son, your sins are forgiven" (Mark 2:5). Though the physical cure is amazing, it is this spiritual response that affirms that Jesus is God, for only God has the power to forgive sins.

In the Gospels, Jesus heals several blind men. One healing in particular has significance in that it includes a confrontation with the religious leaders. They question whether the man's blindness is the result of his sins or the sins of his parents. Continually finding fault in Jesus, these religious leaders assume that anyone who heals on the Sabbath (which is when the healing takes place) cannot be of God. This healing story allows us to see beyond the obvious to the core of Jesus' teachings. Jesus acts out of a spirit of love and compassion rather than religious laws and regulations.

Our God is a God of healing, which we see clearly in the ministry of Jesus. Not only does Jesus heal people with physical or emotional injuries, he also transforms people who witness his miracles.

This Chapter at a Glance

Getting to Know the Story of Jesus the Healer

- The Healing Miracles of Jesus

Getting to Know Jesus the Healer

- It's a Matter of Faith

Scripture Passages Related to Jesus the Healer

The passages listed in bold are readings the students will reference to complete the puzzle "Jesus the Healer" on page 21 of the *Student Activity Workbook for "Breakthrough! The Bible for Young Catholics": Getting to Know Jesus.*

- Matthew 8:1-4, **Mark 1:40–45,** Luke 5:12-16 (Jesus heals a man.)
- **Matthew 8:5–13,** Luke 7:1-10 (Jesus heals a Roman officer's servant.)*
- Matthew 8:14-17, **Mark 1:29–34,** Luke 4:38-41 (Jesus heals many people at Peter's house.)
- Matthew 8:28-34, Mark 5:1-20, Luke 8:26-39 (Jesus heals a man with demons.)
- Matthew 9:1-8, **Mark 2:1–12,** Luke 5:17-26 (Jesus heals a paralytic.)*
- Matthew 9:20-22, **Mark 5:21–43,** Luke 8:43-48 (Jesus heals a woman with bleeding and a girl.)
- **Matthew 12:9–13,** Mark 3:1-5, Luke 6:6-11 (Jesus heals a paralyzed man.)
- Matthew 17:14-21, **Mark 9:14–29,** Luke 9:37-43 (Jesus heals a boy with an evil spirit.)
- Matthew 20:29-34, Mark 10:46-52, **Luke 18:35–43** (Jesus heals a blind beggar.)
- Mark 1:21-28, **Luke 4:31–37** (A man with an evil spirit)
- John 4:46-54 (Jesus heals an official's son.)
- **John 5:1–18** (The healing at the pool)*

Asterisk (*) signifies key passages to cover.

BreakThrough!

Articles from *Breakthrough!* Related to Jesus the Healer

- Miracles (Matthew, chapter 8)
- Friends to the Rescue (Matthew 9:1–8)
- The Blind Can See (Matthew 11:1–6)
- Thanks a Lot (Luke 17:11–19)
- Help Me Believe (John 4:46–54)
- Working Together (John 5:1–18)

Jesus the Healer and Young Adolescents Today

- Jesus heals young people, such as the daughter of Jairus and the boy with epilepsy, the official's son at Capernaum. These stories can remind young people that Jesus has great love and concern for people their age.
- Jesus heals people experiencing emotional illness. Young adolescents are in a physical period in their lives when hormones are raging and emotional ups and downs can cause them much concern. These stories of healing can offer them strength and comfort.
- Jesus' concern for ill people can bring comfort to some students who may be concerned about sick family members or friends.
- The Pharisees try to condemn Jesus for breaking the religious laws of the day when he heals on the Sabbath. Young people often question different laws, secular and religious.
- Jesus heals many sick people because of their faith. Young people can see that faith is an essential ingredient to prayers of petition.

Getting to Know the Story of Jesus the Healer

The Healing Miracles of Jesus

In this activity the students explore the healing miracles of Jesus and report their findings to the class.

Preparation

- ❑ Make copies of handout 7–A, "Exploring the Healing Miracles," one for each young person.
- ❑ Provide each student with a copy of *Breakthrough! The Bible for Young Catholics* or another Bible and a pen or pencil.

1. Distribute handout 7-A, the bibles, and the pens or pencils. Assign a healing miracle from the handout to each young person to explore. Review the handout questions and then ask each student to answer them in light of their miracle story.

2. When the students have finished researching their assigned miracles, have them share their findings with the class.

3. Then have the students reflect on what they have heard about Jesus' miracles by discussing these questions:

- What types of people did Jesus heal?
- What did Jesus mention frequently as an essential ingredient to his intervention? *[faith]*
- What was a common reaction from the crowd? *[amazement]*
- How can we apply to our present lives the knowledge we've gained by doing this assignment? *[Stress that we must try to pray with the kind of faith held by the sick people whom Jesus healed.]*

Note: If the young people have the student workbook, they will be well prepared to complete the puzzle "Jesus the Healer" on page 21 after completing this activity. See appendix 2 of this manual for the solution to the puzzle.

Getting to Know Jesus the Healer

It's a Matter of Faith

In this activity the students reflect on their own faith at this time in their lives.

Preparation

- ❑ Provide each student with a copy of *Breakthrough! The Bible for Young Catholics* or another Bible, a sheet of paper, and a pen or pencil.

1. Distribute the bibles, paper, and pens or pencils. Have the students read the following healing accounts quietly to themselves: Luke 7:1–10, Matthew 20:29–34, Mark 5:25–34, and John 4:43–54.

2. After the students have had sufficient time to read the Scripture passages, discuss the essential characteristic that each person displays and that impressed Jesus enough to allow for healing to take place. *[faith]*

3. Next, have the students review each Scripture passage and list reasons as to why they believe each person seeking healing exhibited great faith.

4. Invite the students to quietly think about their own faith life and its ups and downs. Are there activities or people who help reinforce their faith? Are there questions they would like to discuss that might move them forward in their spiritual life? Emphasize that faith is a gift and that any person who would like to grow in faith need only ask God for help.

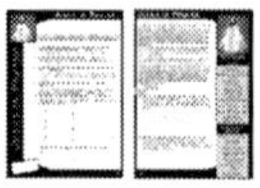

Note: If the young people are using the student workbook, question 1 on page 22 nicely complements this last step. You may want to actually have the young people answer the question in writing and then hold a discussion around the questions in step 4.

Exploring the Healing Miracles

Read one of the following healing stories and then answer the questions below:

Mark 1:40–45 (Jesus Heals a Man)	**Matthew 12:9–13** (Jesus Heals a Paralyzed Man)
Matthew 8:5–13 (Jesus Heals a Roman Officer's Servant)	**Mark 9:14–29** (Jesus Heals a Boy with an Evil Spirit)
Mark 1:29–34 (Jesus Heals Many People)	**Luke 18:35–43** (Jesus Heals a Blind Beggar)
Luke 8:26–39 (Jesus Heals a Man with Demons)	**Luke 4:31–37** (A Man with an Evil Spirit)
Mark 2:1–12 (Jesus Heals a Paralyzed Man)	**John 4:46–54** (Jesus Heals an Official's Son)
Mark 5:21–43 (Jairus's Daughter and the Woman Who Touched Jesus' Cloak)	**John 5:1–18** (Jesus Heals the Man at the Pool)

1. Where does the miracle take place?

2. Who is involved?

3. What is requested of Jesus?

4. What is Jesus' spoken response?

5. What intervention takes place?

6. What is the reaction (if any) of the crowd that is present?

7. What is your reaction to the miracle?

Chapter 8

Getting to Know Jesus the Bread of Life

Preparing to Teach

Overview

Young adolescents appear to be hungry all the time. It is no wonder, as they are growing so much and their bodies are changing rapidly! More than anything else, people need water and food to survive, because these things create and sustain the very cells in our bodies and make every process work. It may not be as obvious to young people that our spirits need just as much nourishment and attention as our bodies or they will waste away in a way that parallels physical starvation.

This chapter explores the ways Jesus feeds people, both physically and spiritually. The stories of the multiplication of bread and fish show Jesus to be a deeply compassionate teacher who always thanks his Father before giving to people. This gratitude is a sign of his fidelity to God the Father. This fidelity is also visible when we see Jesus feed the spiritual needs of others, such as when he attends to the prostitute who interrupts Simon the Pharisee's dinner party or when he spends time with Martha's sister, Mary, who sits with him before preparing the family supper.

Jesus is the Bread of Life. A relationship with Jesus nourishes us and sustains us not just temporarily, but in an ongoing, committed way. The most intimate way Jesus nourishes us is in the Eucharist, but he also does so when we read the Scriptures and pray privately and communally.

In order to follow Jesus, we must feed one another, both physically and spiritually. When we meet the needs of others rather than thinking of ourselves, we are somehow more ourselves even though we are giving something away.

This Chapter at a Glance

Getting to Know the Story of Jesus the Bread of Life

- Loaves and Fishes

Getting to Know Jesus the Bread of Life

- The Feeding of the Five Thousand, Then and Now

Scripture Passages Related to Jesus the Bread of Life

The passages listed in bold are readings the students will reference to complete the puzzle "Jesus the Bread of Life" on page 23 of the *Student Activity Workbook for "Breakthrough! The Bible for Young Catholics": Getting to Know Jesus.*

- Matthew 19:13-15 (Jesus blesses children.)
- Matthew 14:13-21, **Mark 6:30-44,** Luke 9:10-17 (Jesus feeds five thousand.)*
- Matthew 15:32-39, Mark 8:1-10 (Jesus feeds four thousand.)
- Matthew 26:17-30, **Mark 14:12-26,** Luke 22:7-23 (The Lord's Supper)*
- Luke 7:36-50 (Jesus at the home of Simon)
- Luke 10: 38-42 (Martha and Mary)*
- John 6:25-59 (Jesus, the bread of life)*

Asterisk (*) signifies key passages to cover.

Articles from *Breakthrough!* Related to Jesus the Bread of Life

Break Through!

- Feeding the Crowds (Matthew 15:32-39)
- Feeding the Hungry (Mark 6:30-44)
- The Real Deal (Mark 14:22-25)
- Walking with Jesus (Luke 24:13-35)
- The Eucharist Is Central! (John, chapter 6)
- You Snooze, You Lose (Acts 20:7-12)
- The Eucharistic Meal (1 Corinthians 11:23-33)

Jesus the Bread of Life and Young Adolescents Today

- Young adolescents long for real life. Jesus offers them this life in the Eucharist and through a relationship with him based on prayer and reading the Scriptures.

- Young adolescents need to have their spirits nurtured just as they need to have their bodies fed. Jesus offers them this spiritual food.
- Jesus desires to meet young people in the Eucharist. Young people want to be known and loved and can find these needs met through the Eucharist.
- Jesus wants people to join him in feeding others physically and spiritually. Young adolescents can be very generous toward people in need, just as Jesus was to the people who were hungry.

Getting to Know the Story of Jesus the Bread of Life

Loaves and Fishes

In this activity students play a game that familiarizes them with the story of Jesus the Bread of Life.

Preparation

- ❑ Provide copies of *Breakthrough! The Bible for Young Catholics* or another Bible, one for each student.
- ❑ For each group of four students, assemble the following items:
  - a copy of the game board from resource 8-A, *"Loaves and Fishes: A Game of Feeding Others"*
  - enough copies of the loaves and fishes cards from resource 8-B, "Card Template for *Loaves and Fishes: A Game of Feeding Others,*" so that each group has forty cards to start. (You may want to make the copies on card stock if you want to use the games more than once.)
  - game markers, a coin, and some snacks for the winning player (perhaps Goldfish crackers or gummy fish)

1. Divide the class into groups of four and give each group a Bible, a game board, a set of seven loaves and fishes cards, game markers, and a coin. Put the extra loaves and fishes cards next to the board. (This will also be the discard area.)

2. Read Mark 6:30–44 aloud to the young people. Introduce the game with these thoughts:

- ❍ In the miracle of the feeding of the five thousand people, someone comes forward to offer a few loaves and fishes to Jesus so Jesus can reveal himself as the true Bread of Life. The object of this game is to give away all your loaves and fishes so you too can receive the "prize"—Jesus the Bread of Life. The game board is shaped like the nutrition pyramid to remind us that good spiritual nutrition is based on Jesus the Living Bread.

If the young people have the student workbook, you may want to stop here and have them answer question 1 on page 24, which takes the spiritual nutrition pyramid another step by asking the students to come up with a weekly spiritual menu.

3. Give these instructions to the young people:

- Flip the coin to begin the game. A player who gets heads can move one space. A player who receives tails moves two spaces.
- Follow the instructions on each space. Read the Scripture passage together and either pick up or give away a loaves and fishes card.
- Continue this way until the first player reaches the Bread of Life space at the top of the pyramid without any loaves or fishes cards. This person is the winner. Players who reach the top of the pyramid but still have cards should continue to participate in the flow of the game and at their turn, flip a coin to see if they can give away any loaves or fishes cards or if they must keep them. At this point "heads" means they can give away a loaves and fishes card and "tails" means they should keep all their loaves and fishes cards until their next turn.
- All players must lose their loaves and fishes cards before the game is over.

4. Discuss the Scripture passages the students read for the game. Ask how it is that to be the winner, a person has to be in the final space and have no cards left. What does this Christian paradox look like in everyday life?

If the young people have the student workbook, you may want to assign them the puzzle "Jesus the Bread of Life" on page 23, which asks them to reread two important passages—Mark 6:33-44 and Mark 14:22-26—in order to complete the puzzle. See appendix 2 of this manual for the solution to the puzzle.

Getting to Know Jesus the Bread of Life

The Feeding of the Five Thousand, Then and Now

Preparation

- ❑ Provide each student with a copy of *Breakthrough! The Bible for Young Catholics* or another Bible, a sheet of paper, and a pen or pencil.
- ❑ Ideally, invite a speaker from a local food bank or soup kitchen.

1. Introduce the activity with these thoughts:

- The miracle of the feeding of the five thousand continues to happen today in all kinds of ways. The miracle depends on people of faith offering what they have to God and then taking the responsibility of offering these gifts to the poor. Then the miracle truly occurs.

2. Distribute the bibles and ask one student to read Mark 6:30–44 aloud to the group. Ask the students these questions:

- What is the meaning of this event for followers of Jesus?
- How is this similar to the Last Supper?
- Have you witnessed this type of miracle today?
- What is the moral of the accounts of these apparently miraculous events? *[When we offer our little gifts to God in faith for others, miraculous things can happen.]*

3. Have the young people privately reflect on any events in their lives that they consider miracles. Ask these questions:

- Did you pray in that time?
- How did your faith grow?
- How was God close to you even in your weakness and struggle?

Invite the students to share their reflections as they feel comfortable.

4. Share this modern parable on heaven and hell:

- Once a man was trying to imagine the difference between heaven and hell when an angel of God appeared to him and asked if he would like to visit both places to see for himself. The man agreed, so the angel whisked him away. They arrived in a park-like setting with people sitting on either side of a long, long, long banquet table that stretched out as far as the man could see in either direction. On the table the visitor could see bowls heaped with fruits, plates steaming with choice meats and vegetables, and baskets filled with warm bread. But what most struck the visitor was the horrific sound he heard: the sickening moaning and wailing of people starving to death! Each person seated at the table had an extremely long fork or spoon, and no matter how hard they tried, they could not get the food from their plates to their mouths with the implements. As the man walked along, he saw men and women elbowing and threatening each other out of desperation for some food. He saw men and women withered and haggard, their eyes sunken and lips dried out from the effort. Each had decided they were in it for themselves. The visitor turned to the angel and said, "Messenger of God, surely this is hell! Please, show me heaven!"

And so the angel whisked the man off to another park-like setting. And like the previous setting, this one, too, contained a long, long, long banquet table that stretched as far as the visitor could see in either direction. And like the previous place, there were men and women sitting on both sides of table, which was filled with bowls, plates, and baskets of delicious food. And, again, what struck the man was the sound he heard: joyful, hearty, unending laughter, for all the feasters at these tables, though still using the oversized forks and spoons, were feeding each other and were utterly delighted with the feast they had been provided. "So this is heaven," the man said. "It seems both heaven and hell are within our grasp, depending on what we choose."

(This is one version of a common story.)

5. Ask the students to reflect on the moral of the story. If you are able to invite someone in who can discuss current attempts to end hunger, inquire whether that person has any service project ideas for your students.

If the young people have the student workbook, this would be a good time for them to reflect on question 2 on page 24 and discuss it.

Loaves and Fishes: A Game of Feeding Others

END OF THE GAME!

Read John 6:48–56. Besides the Bread of Life, what else does Jesus call himself? If you are out of loaves and fishes cards, you have won! If you still have cards, flip the coin. Heads? Discard ONE card on this turn. Tails? Keep all your cards until it is your next turn.

Read Luke 22:14–20. What does Jesus say at this supper? You share in this meal. Discard ONE card.

Read John 6:35–40. At the Last Supper, you hear Jesus say you will never be thirsty or hungry again. Flip a coin. Heads? You believe it. Discard ONE card. Tails? You are not sure you believe it. Pick up ONE card.

Read Luke 10:38–42. What does Jesus say to Martha? You agree with Jesus and offer some fish for dinner. Discard ONE card.

Read Mark 14:22–26. What event will this dinner be? You bring TWO loaves to the meal. Discard TWO cards.

Read Matthew 26:26–30. On the way to the meal, you pass a poor person but don't give him any food. Pick up ONE card.

Read Luke 7:36–50. What does the woman do? Flip the coin. Heads? You want Jesus to help her. Discard ONE card. Tails? You want her to leave the party. Pick up ONE card.

Read Luke 7:36–50. What does Jesus tell the woman? You offer her some food. Discard ONE card.

Read Luke 10:38–42. Whose house are you visiting? You bring some food for dinner. Discard ONE card.

Read Luke 10:38–42. You also go to see Martha and Mary, but Jesus thinks you are also troubled by too many things. Pick up ONE card.

Start! Read Mark 6:30–44. How many people are you feeding? Flip a coin: Heads? You shared, so discard ONE loaf and fish card. Tails? You didn't share. Pick up ONE card.

Read Matthew14:13–21. What did Jesus ask the Apostles to do? You do it. Discard TWO cards.

Read Luke 9:10–17. You saw all these people and didn't want to share. In fact, you found another loaf and kept it. Pick up ONE card.

Read Mark 8:1–10. What do the Apostles do after this miracle? You help them. Discard TWO cards.

Read Mark 8:1–10. How many extra baskets of food do you have now? Flip the coin again. Heads? You give away a basket to a family. Discard ONE card. Tails? You keep it for yourself. Pick up ONE card.

Card Template for *Loaves and Fishes: A Game of Feeding Others*

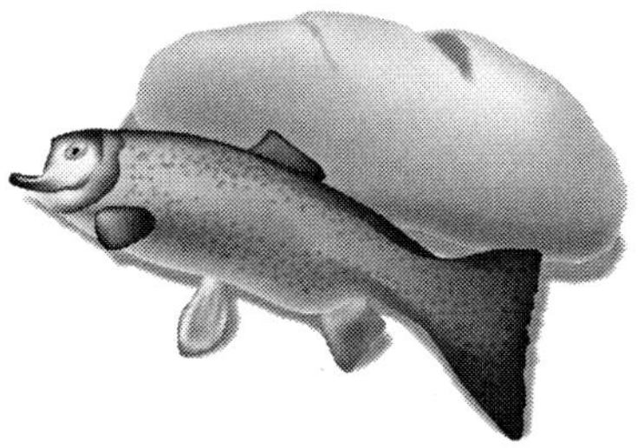
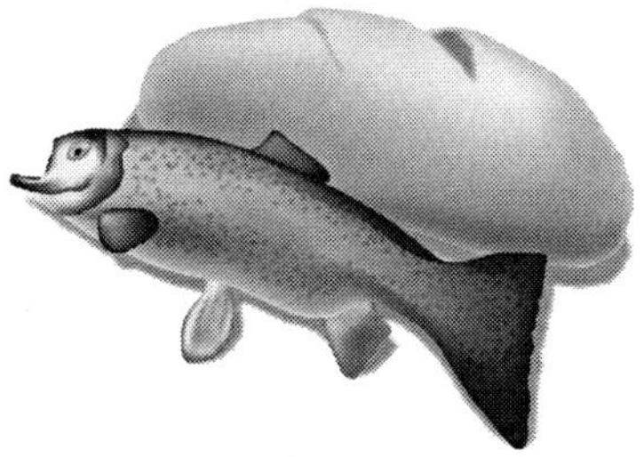
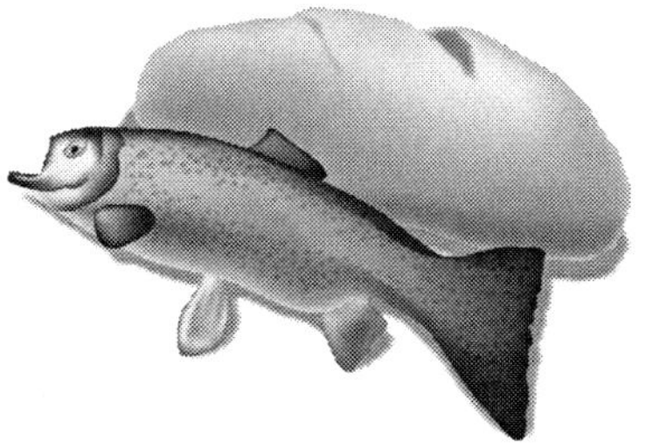
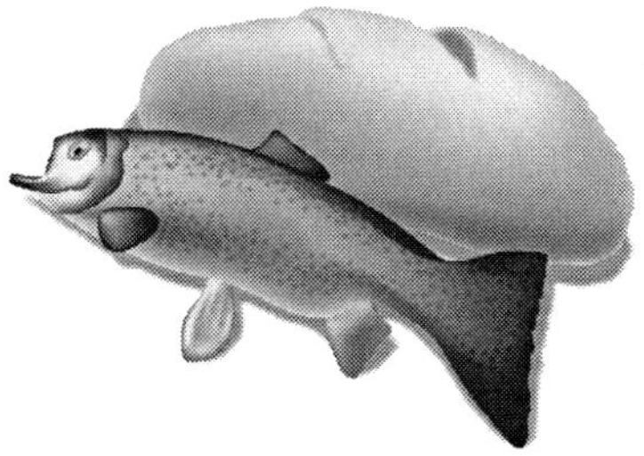
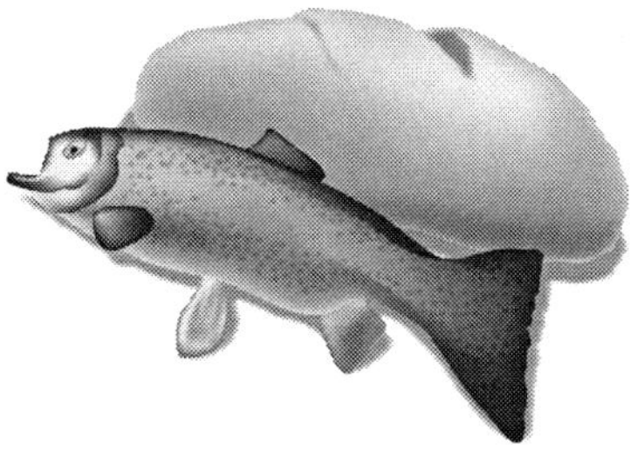
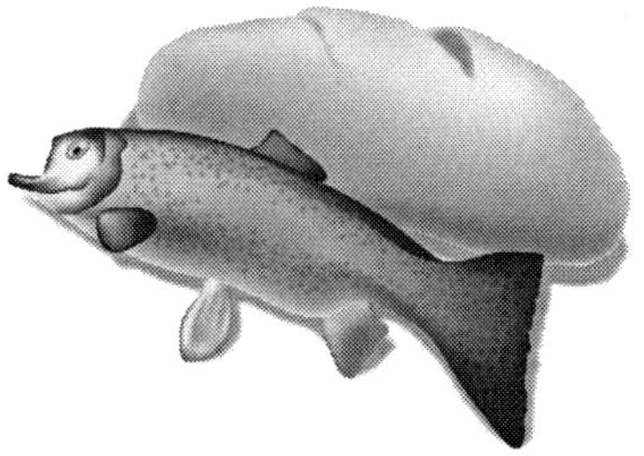
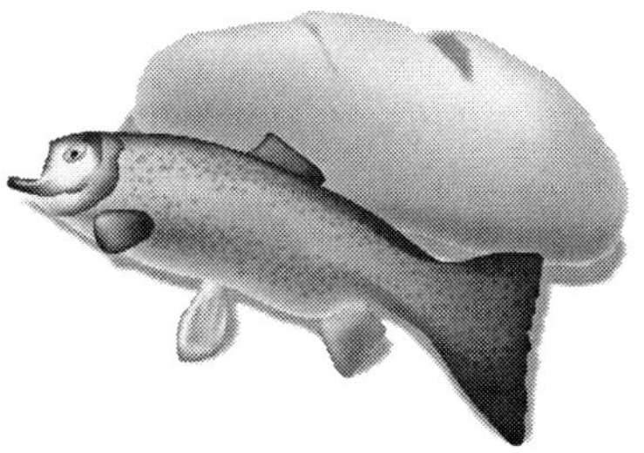
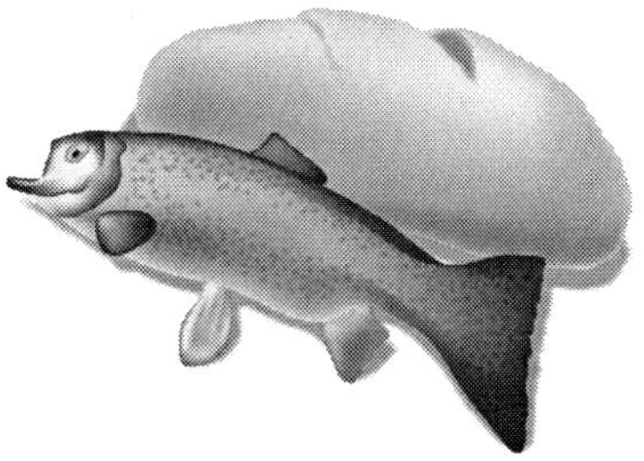

Chapter 9

Getting to know Jesus the Person of Courage

Preparing to Teach

Overview

Young people prefer to be considered courageous rather than fearful, yet oftentimes our culture delivers a message about courage and fear that is different from the one we receive from Jesus. Courage does not mean bravado or being willing to try things that are dangerous, like in some of the reality TV shows. In "real" reality, courage involves choosing Christ-centered values and holding to those convictions even under trying and painful circumstances, whether that be risking the anger of a friend or facing death.

Roughly half of the Gospel of Mark is devoted to the last week of Jesus' life. There is increasing tension between Jesus and the religious authorities in the days leading up to his death. Jesus enters Jerusalem in an effort to share his message with the people of the Jews' spiritual capital. He enters the city riding a colt. The inhabitants of Jerusalem lay their cloaks on the ground and wave palm branches, cheering loudly as if honoring a military hero. As the Pharisees look on with much concern, they become incensed by the outpouring of support Jesus receives. They even ask Jesus to silence the chanting crowd. Jesus replies that "if they keep quiet, the stones themselves will start shouting" (Luke 19:40).

In the garden at Gethsemane, Jesus confides in Peter, James, and John that he is filled with anxiety. Jesus cries out to his Father to remove his suffering yet affirms his commitment to the will of God by his words: "Yet not what I want, but what you want" (Mark 14:36). The humanity of Jesus is never made more apparent than at this very moment. How disappointed Jesus must be when he asks the disciples to remain awake with him in his hour of need and he finds them asleep.

Courage in Christ requires a spiritual vigilance that Jesus' friends cannot muster that night in the garden. Courageous Catholics ask Jesus to nourish them through the Eucharist, prayer, and supportive friendships.

This Chapter at a Glance

Getting to Know the Story of Jesus the Person of Courage

- Jesus Is Arrested and Sentenced to Death!

Getting to Know Jesus the Person of Courage

- Different Perspectives

Chapter 9

Scripture Passages Related to Jesus the Person of Courage

The passages listed in bold are readings the students will reference to complete the puzzle "Jesus the Person of Courage" on page 25 of the *Student Activity Workbook for "Breakthrough! The Bible for Young Catholics": Getting to Know Jesus.*

- Matthew 16:21-28, Mark 8:31-38, Luke 9:22-27 (Jesus speaks about his suffering and death.)
- Matthew 20:17-19, Mark 10:32-34, Luke 18:31-34 (Jesus speaks a third time about his death.)
- Matthew 21:1-11, Mark 11:1-11, **Luke19:28–40,** John 12:12-19 (The triumphant entry into Jerusalem)*
- Matthew 26:36-56, **Mark 14:32–52**, Luke 22:39-53 (Jesus prays in Gethsemane.)*
- **Matthew 26:14–16,47–56**; Luke 22:3-6,47-53; John 13:21-30, 18:1-5 (Judas's betrayal of Jesus)*
- Matthew 26:69-75, Mark 14:66-72, **Luke 22:54–62** (Peter's denial of Jesus)*
- Matthew 26:57-68; Mark 14:53-65; Luke 22:54,66-71 (Jesus before the Council)
- Matthew 27:1-2, Luke 23:1-5, John 18:28-33 (Jesus before Pilate)
- Matthew 27:15-26, Mark 15:6-15, Luke 23:13-25, **John 18:39—19:16** (Jesus is sentenced to death.)*

Asterisk (*) signifies key passages to cover.

Articles from *Breakthrough!* Related to Jesus the Person of Courage

Break Through!

- What She Has Done (Matthew 26:6-13)
- Obstacles to Prayer (Matthew 26:36-46)

- I Messed Up Again, Jesus (Mark 14:32–72)
- An Act of Courage (Mark 15:42–47)
- It Wasn't Me! (Luke 22:54–62)

Jesus the Person of Courage and Young Adolescents Today

- Jesus shares his feelings and concerns with the disciples when he tells them about his eventual death. Students share the intimate details about their lives with those who are closest to them.
- When Jesus enters Jerusalem, he is hailed as king yet remains humble and focused on his ministry. Students experience times in their lives when they are praised and admired. These experiences may sometimes cloud their ability to remain humble. The example Jesus models can remind them to avoid being show-offs.
- Jesus experiences stress and extreme anxiety in the garden at Gethsemane. Young adolescents are constantly exposed to stress and anxiety-provoking events. Staying close to God in prayer helps them overcome overwhelming fears that can develop.
- Judas Iscariot, a disciple of Jesus, eventually betrays him. Sometimes young adolescents are not loyal to their friends.
- Peter denies knowing Jesus, yet Jesus forgives him. Jesus' love for young people is so great that he is willing to forgive them and us when we deny him by our sinful actions.
- Jesus continues to speak the truth even though he knows he will face death. Sometimes students need to stand up for the truth regardless of the consequences.

Getting to Know the Story of Jesus the Person of Courage

Jesus Is Arrested and Sentenced to Death!

In this activity the students use the Scriptures to identify the facts surrounding the arrest and sentencing of Jesus. If your students are using the workbook, you may want to do this activity with them and then have them complete the puzzle "Jesus the Person of Courage" on page 25 as a short review. See appendix 2 of this manual for the solution to the puzzle.

Preparations

- ❑ Provide each student with a copy of *Breakthrough! The Bible for Young Catholics* or another Bible, a sheet of paper, and a pen or pencil.
- ❑ Make copies of handout 9-A, "Jesus' Arrest and Sentencing," one for each student.

1. Divide the class into three groups and assign each group a different Gospel account of the arrest and trial of Jesus. Distribute the bibles, paper, pens or pencils, and handouts.

2. Write the following information on the blackboard:

- **Group 1.** Matthew 26:47–68; 27:1,2,11–26
- **Group 2.** Mark 14:43–65; 15:1–15
- **Group 3.** Luke 22:47–55,63–71; 23:1–5,13–25

3. Allow the students time to answer the questions on the handout. Note that although groups will be able to answer most questions, there will be some that can be answered by only one or two Gospels. Conclude the activity by comparing the four different accounts of Jesus' arrest and trial. Ask the young people to identify aspects of this story that highlight Jesus' courage.

Answers to handout 9–A:

1. Judas
2. a kiss
3. high priest's slave
4. high priest or Caiaphas
5. evidence or witnesses
6. lies (in Matthew and Mark)
7. "I am" (Mark); "So you say" (Matthew and Luke)
8. blasphemy (Matthew and Mark); misleading the people, telling them not to pay taxes, claiming to be the messiah (Luke)
9. Pilate
10. "Are you the king of the Jews?"
11. "So you say" (Matthew and Luke); silence (Mark)
12. Barabbas
13. three
14. to prevent a riot (Matthew); to please the crowd (Mark); because of shouting (Luke)

4. Read John 18:3–14,19–24; 18:28–39; 19:16 with the students and compare John's account with those from the synoptic Gospels.

Note: If the young people are also using the student workbook, review the "Introduction to the Gospels" on pages 5–6.

Getting to Know Jesus the Person of Courage

Different Perspectives

In this activity the students conduct an interview with two biblical characters that play a significant role in sentencing Jesus to death as well as with Jesus' followers.

Preparation

- ❑ Provide each student with a copy of *Breakthrough! The Bible for Young Catholics* or another Bible, a sheet of paper, and a pen or pencil.
- ❑ Arrange the room with four chairs in the front.

1. Divide the class into groups of four. Introduce the next activity with these thoughts in your own words:

- ❍ Few people would disagree that Jesus is a person of courage. A more subtle description of Jesus, however, is that he is a person of integrity. In math an integer is a whole number. A person of integrity is one who is similarly undivided in his or her focus and values, who is completely honest—"what you see is what you get." In this next activity, I would like you to read over the stories from Gethsemane and the sentencing from Caiaphas and Pilate and create a television interview.

Each interview should have two talk show hosts and two biblical figures. Be creative in your presentation and in presenting the viewpoints that these different observers may have had:

- Peter and James, the son of Zebedee (see Matt. 26:37)
- Pilate and Caiaphas
- Two Roman guards
- Two bystanders

2. Give the students sufficient time in class to compose a 5-minute interview featuring two hosts and two disciples as participants. Note that in the interview, the "disciples" can draw on times in Jesus' life other than his Passion to support their position if they wish, but the main focus should remain on the last day of Jesus' life.

If the young people are using the student workbook, answering questions 1 and 2 on page 26 in writing provides an opportunity for them to reflect about the person of Jesus prior to creating the interview.

3. Give each group an opportunity to present its interview and jot down some notes about the examples the groups use to describe Jesus as a person of integrity. Afterward, use this list to help the students extrapolate what a person of integrity would look like in a young adolescent.

Jesus' Arrest and Sentencing

Use the assigned Scripture passages to fill in the answers to the following questions:

1. What is the name of the disciple who betrayed Jesus?
2. What does this disciple use as a signal to betray Jesus?
3. Whose ear is cut off during the arrest of Jesus?
4. Whose house is Jesus taken to?
5. What does the council need in order to put Jesus to death?
6. The witnesses cannot make their stories agree, so what do they tell?
7. What does Jesus answer when the high priest asks if he is the Messiah, the Son of God?
8. What does the high priest accuse Jesus of committing?
9. To whom is Jesus taken next?
10. What question does this man ask of Jesus?
11. How does Jesus answer his question?
12. What is the name of the man set free in place of Jesus?
13. How many times does Pilate try to set Jesus free?
14. Why does Pilate condemn Jesus to death?

Chapter 10

Getting to Know Jesus and His Suffering

Preparing to Teach

Overview

Modern culture, which has been called a culture of death, values life in a very different way than Jesus does and portrays suffering and death as dead-end streets. To live the reality of the Paschal mystery is to see the world in a much different way. Though understanding our own lives in light of the Paschal mystery does not make suffering fun, it does give a redemptive meaning to it. If we unite our suffering with Christ's suffering on the cross, he will change us and bring us true life.

The Paschal mystery fully reveals God and his perfect love for us. God's mercy redeems humanity from *all* sin and transforms it. After the Resurrection, sin and death, though still at work in the world, have also been overcome by God's grace. Through Christ's sacrificial love, all people now share in this Paschal mystery and all of life has been permanently renewed.

Young people who can begin to see suffering and death through the eyes of faith have taken a significant step in their faith journeys.

This Chapter at a Glance

Getting to Know the Story of Jesus and His Suffering

- The Stations of the Cross from Mark, Matthew, and Luke

Getting to Know Jesus and His Suffering

- "The Last Words of Jesus": A CD Cover Design
- The Power of Sacrificial Love

Scripture Passages Related to Jesus and His Suffering

The passages listed in bold are readings the students will reference to complete the puzzle "Jesus and His Suffering on puzzle on page 27 of the *Student Activity Workbook for "Breakthrough! The Bible for Young Catholics": Getting to Know Jesus.*

- Matthew 27:26-31, **Mark 15:16–20,** John 19:1-3 (Jesus is whipped.)*
- **Mark 15:21,** John 19:17 (The walk to Calvary)*
- Luke 23:26-32 (Simon helps carry the cross; Jesus meets women.)
- Matthew 27:33-38, **Mark 15:22–28,** Luke 23:33-38, John 19:18-27 (Jesus is crucified.)*
- Matthew 27:39-44, **Mark 15:29–36** (Jesus is taunted.)
- Luke 23:39-43 (Jesus speaks with the good thief.)
- Matthew 27:45-50, **Mark 15:37–41,** Luke 23:44-46, John 19:28-37 (Jesus' death)*
- Matthew 27:51-56 (Earthquake)
- Luke 23:47-49 (People express sorrow at Jesus' death.)
- Matthew 27:57-66, **Mark 15:42–47,** Luke 23:50-56, John 19:38-42 (Jesus' burial)*

Asterisk (*) signifies key passages to cover.

Break Through!

Articles from *Breakthrough!* Related to Jesus and His Suffering

- Good Friday (Matthew 26:57—27:56)
- Thank You, Lord (Matthew 27:32-50)
- Jesus, Remember Me! (Luke 23:39-43)
- Our Family (John 19:25-27)

Jesus and His Suffering and Young Adolescents Today

- In dying, Jesus makes a sacrifice for all of humanity. Young adolescents are familiar with the idea of sacrifice, having done so themselves for friends or family or by experiencing the sacrifice of others for them.
- Jesus' suffering is the Paschal mystery that saves humanity. Young adolescents may interpret from our culture's messages that suffering has no value. In the Christian Catholic worldview, suffering always has value when we suffer with Christ.
- In these readings, we see the grief that others experienced because Jesus died. Just as the Resurrection surpassed Jesus' death, young people can understand that hope in the Paschal mystery is also possible for them when they grieve.

Getting to Know the Story of Jesus and His Suffering

The Stations of the Cross from Mark, Matthew, and Luke

In this activity the students create and illustrate an adapted stations of the cross.

If the young people are using the student workbook and you are short on time, you might want them to answer question 1 on page 28, invite discussion, and then go directly to step 6 of this activity.

Preparation

- ❑ Provide markers, newsprint, and masking tape for each of three small groups.
- ❑ Provide copies of *Breakthrough! The Bible for Young Catholics* or another Bible, one for each student.

1. Begin the activity by asking the young people to reflect on the nature and meaning of the stations of the cross. Students may respond by saying this devotion is a prayerful way to commemorate fourteen different aspects of Jesus' suffering and death. Explain that this prayer developed as a way to help people identify with the suffering and death of Jesus. Since then it has become a popular devotion.

2. Tell the students they will be creating several versions of the stations of the cross. Divide the class into three groups and give each group at least seven sheets of newsprint in addition to markers and masking tape. (Have some extra newsprint ready in case the young people are able to do more stations.)

3. Distribute the bibles. Assign each group one of the Passion narratives from Matthew, Mark, or Luke, and have the group as a whole review the Passion narrative in their particular Gospel. Give these additional instructions:

- ❍ Each group should create a series of pictures on newsprint that narrates Jesus' suffering and death. You do not need to make fourteen stations, but each person in your group should illustrate at least one station on a piece of newsprint and no group should leave out an important element of the Passion story from their Gospel.
- ❍ Each sheet of newsprint should have a quote from the Scriptures that is related to the image, large enough to read from a short distance.

4. As each group finishes its stations, have its members display their images on the walls of the classroom with masking tape. When all the images have been completed, assemble them by theme so that, for example, all the "scourging" images are grouped together, all the "walk to Calvary" images are grouped together, and so on. Ask the young people to notice the similarities and differences between the stations within a grouping.

5. When the groups are done creating their stations of the cross, pray it with them. Begin with the sign of the cross, and as you announce each grouping's title (for example, "Jesus is whipped"), have the students who prepared that station read the Scriptures from their pictures. Say the Lord's Prayer and a Hail Mary after each station grouping.

6. Afterward discuss the meaning of the Paschal (or Easter) mystery with the students. Talk about the outcome of Jesus' suffering, which was not death but new life. Relate the connection between suffering in everyday life and the Resurrection by giving the students some concrete examples of ways life can come out of painful situations. Note that our culture often tells us we should avoid suffering (at all costs) and aging (at all costs) but that this perspective is based on fear and reflects the success of some marketing campaigns for pain-relief and beauty products.

Distinguish, however, between the value of sacrifice (to make holy) and suffering, and the misperception that suffering is to be desired. Note that suffering came into the world through original sin and was not part of God's original plan for us. Just because suffering can bring new life does not mean we should seek it out; rather it means we should go to God with it when it comes to us.

Getting to Know Jesus and His Suffering

"The Last Words of Jesus": A CD Cover Design

In this activity the young people look at Jesus' final words and create songs to go with them.

If the young people are using the student workbook and you are short on time, ask them to answer question 2 on page 28 to explore the kind of love Jesus demonstrates through his death.

Preparation

- ❑ Provide copies of *Breakthrough! The Bible for Young Catholics* or another Bible, one for each student.

- ❑ Make copies of handouts 10-A, "The Last Words of Jesus," and 10-B, "CD Cover Template," one of each for each young person. Also provide scissors, markers, or colored pens. You may want to give each student two CD cover templates so they can use one as a rough draft.

1. Have the students reflect on an experience of being saved, defended, protected from harm, healed, or rescued by someone. Ask these questions:

- Did this saving or rescue involve sacrifice on someone's part? If so, how?
- How does Jesus approach his task of saving us from sin and death? Why does he willingly go through with it despite the sacrifice?

2. Distribute handouts 10-A, "The Last Words of Jesus," and 10-B, "CD Cover Template," and the other art materials. Read through the directions on handout 10-A with the young people.

3. When all the students have finished the assignment, invite them to look at one another's CD covers. Have a few students read some of their song lyrics to the class.

The Power of Sacrificial Love

In this activity the students look at *The Lion, the Witch and the Wardrobe* in light of the story of Jesus' suffering, death, and Resurrection.

Preparation

- ❑ Provide a sheet of paper and a pen or pencil for each student.
- ❑ Obtain a copy of the DVD *The Chronicles of Narnia: The Lion, the Witch and the Wardrobe* (2005, 143 minutes, rated PG) and have a DVD player and TV monitor ready.

1. Introduce the activity by asking the students if they have read or seen a stage production of C. S. Lewis's *The Lion, the Witch and the Wardrobe,* or if they have seen the movie *The Chronicles of Narnia: The Lion, the Witch and the Wardrobe.*

If they have, ask them to take turns telling the story and naming the main characters. (If most of the students have not read the book or seen the movie, show parts of the film for the class.)

2. Compare aspects of *The Lion, the Witch and the Wardrobe* with the Passion and death of Jesus by asking these questions:

- What is the prophecy that will redeem Narnia?
- Why is it "always winter but never Christmas" in Narnia?
- Why must Aslan die?
- How does Aslan explain to the girls his coming back to life?

3. Now that the students have processed the story itself, have them discuss ways the story helps us gain insight into the Paschal mystery.

The Last Words of Jesus

Directions: Read the following seven Scripture passages that each contain one of the seven last words (meaning phrases or statements) of Jesus. Create a song title for each Scripture passage, expressing what you think these last statements meant to Jesus. Choose one song title and write out the lyrics for the song.

- Mark 15:33–36
- Luke 23:32–34
- Luke 23:39–43
- Luke 23:44–45
- John 19:25–27
- John 19:28
- John 19:29–30

1. Create a front cover for your CD. Title it *The Last Words of Jesus.*

2. On the back cover of the CD, list the seven song titles you have written.

3. On the inside of the CD cover, write the lyrics of your song. The lyrics should express what you think Jesus was feeling in this scene. Use more paper if you need to.

4. Feel free to add additional material to the CD cover, such as the record company, special thanks, and so on.

CD Cover Template

Chapter 11

Getting to Know the Risen Jesus

Preparing to Teach

Overview

The stories of the Resurrection are among the most beautiful in the Gospels. Crushed followers who have been mourning the death of their beloved Jesus see him and talk with him again! Not only is Jesus still alive, but all that he promised is true too!

One of the most senseless and painful events in people's lives is the death of a young person. Whether this death is from cancer, a car accident, or a random and strange illness, the death of a person with so much potential and life within goes against our sense of what is just.

The promise of eternal life is about the only hope that helps people of any age get through such a loss. After the initial months and years have passed, those closest to this person may say they feel like they already have one foot in heaven, like they can still feel the child's presence, or like they have a glimpse of eternal life now. These experiences testify to the reality of the Resurrection in our midst.

We cannot emphasize too much to young adolescents how important the Resurrection is, how different a life without this type of hope is from one that lives in the hope of resurrection. Not only is death not "the end," but suffering is not meaningless; each person has an eternal destiny of life with God, and this life is not the only measure by which all decisions should be considered.

Be aware that the young people before you may have experienced the loss of people close to them, some recently. Though resurrection is hope for all of us, we must be careful to speak of resurrection in light of the whole Paschal mystery—suffering and dying as well.

This Chapter at a Glance

Getting to Know the Story of the Risen Jesus

- Appearances of the Risen Jesus

Getting to Know the Risen Jesus

- It Is Not Always Easy to Recognize Jesus

Scripture Passages Related to the Risen Jesus

The passages listed in bold are nearly all the readings the students will reference to complete the puzzle "The Risen Jesus" on page 29 of the *Student Activity Workbook for "Breakthrough! The Bible for Young Catholics": Getting to Know Jesus.*

- **Matthew 28:1–10, Mark 16:1–10, Luke 24:1–12,** John 20:1–10 (The Resurrection)*
- **Matthew 28:11–15** (The report of the guard)
- Mark 16:12–13, **Luke 24:13–35** (The walk to Emmaus)*
- Matthew 28:16–20, Mark 16:14–18, **Luke 24:36–49,** John 20:19–23, Acts 1:6–8 (Jesus appears to his disciples.)*
- Matthew 28:9–10, Mark 16:9–11, **John 20:11–18** (Jesus appears to Mary Magdalene.)*
- **John 20:24–29** (Jesus and Thomas)
- **John 21:1–14** (Jesus appears to seven disciples.)*
- **John 21:15–19** (Jesus and Peter)
- Mark 16:19–20, **Luke 24:50–52,** Acts 1:6–11 (Jesus is taken up to heaven.)*

Asterisk (*) signifies key passages to cover.

Articles from *Breakthrough!* Related to the Risen Jesus

- Holy Trinity (Matthew 28:16–20)
- A Model Friend (Mark 16:1–11)
- Celebrate Easter (Luke 24:1–12)
- Walking with Jesus (Luke 24:13–35)
- Peace (John 20:19–21)
- Penance and Reconciliation (John 20:19–23)
- Apostolic Succession (John 21:15–19)
- Now What? (Acts 1:1–11)

The Risen Jesus and Young Adolescents Today

- Jesus appears first to Mary Magdalene, which is testimony of his desire to save all people, no matter their role in society. Young adolescents are often more accepting of people with differences and can be less concerned with social distinctions than their parents and grandparents.
- Jesus appears to two disciples on the way to Emmaus, but they fail to recognize him at once. Jesus also wants to reveal himself to young adolescents, but they do not always recognize him.
- When Jesus asks Peter three times if he loves him, he is offering Peter a chance to overcome his spiritual failures. Young

adolescents are given that same chance when they receive the sacrament of Penance and Reconciliation.

- Before he ascends into heaven, Jesus promises he will remain with his followers in spirit. Young people are offered this same promise.
- Jesus is clear in establishing his mission for the Church. All young adolescent Christians have a responsibility to carry out that mission, especially those who have received the sacrament of Confirmation.

Getting to Know the Story of the Risen Jesus

Appearances of the Risen Jesus

In this activity the students match Scripture citations with corresponding stories of the appearance of the risen Jesus.

If the young people have the student workbook, they can also complete the puzzle "The Risen Jesus" on page 29. Both of these activities ask the young people to read fairly comprehensively, and each activity could be done alone or as a review of the other. See appendix 2 of this manual for the solution to the puzzle.

Preparation

- ❑ Provide each student with a copy of *Breakthrough! The Bible for Young Catholics* or another Bible, a sheet of paper, and a pen or pencil.
- ❑ Make copies of handout 11-A, "Appearances of the Risen Jesus," one for each student.

1. Distribute the bibles, the handouts, and the pens or pencils. Allow the students time to individually complete the handout.

2. When the students have completed the handout, review the following answers with them:
Answers to handout 11-A: 1—D, 2—G, 3—I, 4—A, 5—J, 6—B, 7—H, 8—F, 9—C, 10—E

3. Conclude the activity by discussing the following questions:

- ❍ Why did Jesus appear to so many?
- ❍ What was his message?
- ❍ Why is this important to us today?

- ❍ Which story is your favorite? Why?
- ❍ What are some of the differences you notice between Jesus *before* his death and Resurrection and *after*?

If the young people have the student workbook, you may want them to answer question 1 on page 30 as a way for them to reflect on the joy that these encounters with Jesus brought.

Getting to Know the Risen Jesus

It Is Not Always Easy to Recognize Jesus

Though the disciples are actually walking with Jesus on the way to Emmaus, they do not recognize him until he breaks bread with them. In this activity the young people reflect on the roadblocks they encounter to recognizing Jesus.

1. Have the students read the story "The Walk to Emmaus," Luke 24:13–35, quietly to themselves or for homework. Ask one student to proclaim this Gospel reading to the class.

2. Ask the young people to spend time journaling about these questions:

- ❍ Is there a time you put aside each day to spend with Jesus?
- ❍ If not, does your life seem too busy for Jesus?
- ❍ Can we lose sight of Jesus if we don't spend time with him in prayer?

Discuss everyday schedules with the students. Compare the story "The Walk to Emmaus" to our everyday lives, and ask the students how we can find Jesus in our everyday lives—in nature, in social outreach programs, or in the quiet of our hearts.

If you are using the student workbook, you may want to have the young people answer question 2 on page 30 in writing.

3. Conclude by compiling a written list of suggestions, given by the class, for spending time with students. Encourage the students to choose one suggestion and put it into practice.

APPEARANCES OF THE RISEN JESUS

Match the subject matter of the Scripture passage with its corresponding citation.

_____ 1. Mary Magdalene	A. 1 Corinthians 15:5
_____ 2. women disciples	B. John 20:26–29
_____ 3. Emmaus walkers	C. 1 Corinthians 15:7
_____ 4. Peter	D. Mark 16:9
_____ 5. eleven disciples	E. Acts 1:9–12
_____ 6. Thomas and disciples	F. 1 Corinthians 15:6
_____ 7. disciples at Lake Tiberias	G. Matthew 28:1–10
_____ 8. 500	H. John 21:1–14
_____ 9. James	I. Luke 24:13–35
_____ 10. Ascension witnesses	J. Matthew 28:16–20

Chapter 12

Getting to Know Images of Jesus in the Letters

Preparing to Teach

Overview

We live in a visual culture. We see many more images every day than we probably realize. The Church began in a time when many people could not read. Visual images helped early Christians understand complex realities much like stained-glass windows taught people about their faith centuries later.

Many of the words used to describe Jesus and what he did are symbolic, are rich with meaning, and enable the reader to ponder what exactly a statement means. But because of their ability to reveal complexity, they work well today for adults and young people as starting points for trying to understand the mysteries of faith.

The variety of images or metaphors used in the Scriptures of those early Christian communities show us how Jesus was understood in the early Church. In addition, when looked at together, the images display the multiple ways the Church interpreted itself in relation to Christ's salvific work in the world. This chapter reviews the meaning of a few of those images both for the early Church and for us today.

This Chapter at a Glance

Getting to Know the Story of Images of Jesus in the Letters

- Jesus Bumper Stickers

Getting to Know Images of Jesus in the Letters

- Images of Jesus Drawing Book

Scripture Passages Related to Images of Jesus in the Letters

The passages listed in bold are readings the students will reference to complete the puzzle "Images of Jesus in the Letters" on page 31 of the *Student Activities Workbook for "Breakthrough! The Bible for Young Catholics": Getting to Know Jesus.*

- **Romans 8:1–6** (Life in the Spirit)*
- **Romans 8:31–39** (God's love in Christ Jesus)
- **1 Corinthians 12:12–31** (One body with many parts)*
- **2 Corinthians 5:16–19** (new in Christ)
- **Ephesians 2:20** (Cornerstone of the Church)
- **Colossians 1:15–20** (Christ is the visible likeness of the invisible God.)*
- **Colossians 2:6–7** (Fullness of life in Christ)
- **Colossians 2:20—3:4** (Dying and living with Christ)*
- **Hebrews 4:14—5:10** (Jesus is the high priest.)
- **1 Peter 1:19** (Lamb of God)
- **1 John 1:1–4** (Jesus is the word of Life.)
- **1 John 4:14** (Jesus is the savior of the world.)*

Asterisk (*) signifies key passages to cover.

Articles from *Breakthrough!* Related to Images of Jesus in the Letters

Break Through!

- The Eucharistic Meal (1 Corinthians 11:23-33)
- Who Is Equal? (Galatians 3:26–29)
- True God and True Man (Philippians 2:5–11)
- God Is Love (1 John 4:7–21)
- Live in the Light (1 John 1:5–7)
- He Came as a Human Being (2 John)
- The Lamb of God (Revelation, chapter 5)

Images of Jesus in the Letters and Young Adolescents Today

- Young adolescents are visually oriented; presenting images of Jesus in the Letters can help the students understand the relationship between the community of faith and the resurrected Jesus.
- Young adolescents might relate to other images of Jesus than those presented in the New Testament letters. Show the students that these images are reflections of different aspects of Jesus and that other images of Jesus can provide further insights into the relationship between Jesus and the Church.

Getting to Know the Story of Images of Jesus in the Letters

Jesus Bumper Stickers

In this activity the young people share the images of Jesus from the Letters with one another in the form of bumper stickers.

If the young people are using the student workbook and you are short on time or would like a different way to familiarize the students with the images of Jesus, have them complete the puzzle "Images of Jesus in the Letters" on page 31. See appendix 2 of this manual for the solution to the puzzle.

Preparation

- ❑ Provide copies of the readings, sheets of paper, and colored pens or pencils for each student. Either post the readings in a visible place or make copies of handout 12-A, "The Images of Jesus Book," for the students.
- ❑ Provide copies of *Breakthrough! The Bible for Young Catholics* or another Bible, one for each young person.

1. Put the young people into pairs. Share this information with the students in your own words:

- Paul and the other authors share some fairly complex information about Jesus—who he is and how he relates to the world of the time. Your job is to take the complicated message and convert it into one of the most concise forms of writing: the bumper sticker.

Ask the students to share some examples of appropriate bumper stickers they have seen. Note that these stickers condense their messages, such as "Peace Now!"

2. Pass out the materials you have prepared. Suggest that students fold their papers into a size that more closely resembles a bumper sticker. Give each pair one of the readings from the "Scripture Passages Related to Images of Jesus in the Letters" section.

3. Walk around and help any pairs who are having trouble with the language or references in the letters. Recommend that the students use the type of print and imagery they associate with bumper stickers.

4. When the young people have completed the assignment, ask each pair to present its reading, using its bumper sticker as a means of explaining the key message and providing students with an easier way to remember the images of Jesus in the letters.

Getting to Know Images of Jesus in the Letters

Images of Jesus Drawing Book

In this activity the young people draw the images of Jesus in a book that also includes pictures of their own invention.

If the young people are using the student workbook and you are short on time, direct the students to question 2 on page 32, which invites them to read about Jesus and reflect on one image.

Preparation

- ❑ Make one copy of handout 12-A, "The Images of Jesus Book," and ten copies of handout 12-B, "Images of Jesus" for each student.
- ❑ Provide the students with card stock or other paper for a book cover as well as magazines, scissors, markers, colored pencils, and pens.
- ❑ Provide copies of *Breakthrough! The Bible for Young Catholics* or another Bible, one for each young person.

1. Introduce the activity with these thoughts:

- As he ascended to heaven, Jesus told his Apostles, "And I will be with you always, to the end of the age" (Matthew 28:20). Jesus is present differently now than he was prior to his Resurrection. How can we describe what his presence is like now? The Scriptures give us many images of what Jesus is like now and how we can experience him present with us today. In this project we will explore some of these images and think about new ones.

2. Distribute the supplies, handouts, and bibles. Read over the instructions from handout 12-A, "The Images of Jesus Book," with the students.

3. When the young people have finished their pages, have them make a cover for the book from one or more sheets of paper. Then have them staple the cover page and other pages together.

4. Ask the students to place their books on their desks and then to walk quietly around the classroom and look at other students' books. On a separate piece of paper, have the young people write a paragraph explaining what image helps them see Jesus in the Church and the world best and why.

The Images of Jesus Book

Prior to creating your book, read through the passages below and select seven you like best.

Images of Jesus in the Letters

- Romans 8:1–6 (Life in the Spirit)
- Romans 8:31–39 (God's love in Christ Jesus)
- 1 Corinthians 12:12–31 (One body with many parts)
- 2 Corinthians 5:16–19 (New in Christ)
- Ephesians 2:20 (Cornerstone of the Church)
- Colossians 1:15–20 (Christ is the visible likeness of the invisible God.)
- Colossians 2:6–7 (Fullness of life in Christ)
- Colossians 2:20—3:4 (Dying and living with Christ)
- Hebrews 4:14—5:10 (Jesus is the high priest.)
- 1 Peter 1:19 (Lamb of God)
- 1 John 1:1–4 (Jesus is the word of Life.)
- 1 John 4:14 (Jesus is the savior of the world.)

Directions

1. Create a booklet of drawings around the seven images you chose from the readings.

2. Using copies of handout 12–B, "Images of Jesus," fill in the missing part of the sentence "Jesus is like . . ." with the image you are using. Then draw a picture depicting the image in the space provided. Conclude by finishing the sentence "Jesus is like . . . because . . ." in one or two sentences.

3. After creating seven pages of images based on the Scriptures, continue the same process with three additional images, either of your own choosing or from the Bible.

Images of Jesus

"Jesus is like____

____

____

____

____

____

____

____

____

____

____

____

____

____

because____

____

____."

Appendix 1

Additional Resources

Background Reading and References About the Scriptures

2003 Scripture from Scratch Sourcebook. Cincinnati: St. Anthony Messenger Press, 2003.

Achtemeier, Paul J., ed. *The HarperCollins Bible Dictionary.* San Francisco: HarperSanFrancisco, 1996.

Alter, Robert. *The Art of Biblical Narrative.* New York: Basic Books, 1981.

Bergant, Dianne, ed. *The Collegeville Bible Commentary Based on the New American Bible: Old Testament and New Testament.* Collegeville, MN: Liturgical Press, 1992.

Brown, Raymond E. *An Introduction to the New Testament (Anchor Bible Reference Library).* New York: Doubleday, 1997.

———. *Responses to 101 Questions on the Bible.* New York: Paulist Press, 1990.

Brown, Raymond E., SS, Joseph A. Fitzmyer, and Roland E. Murphy, eds. *The New Jerome Biblical Commentary.* Third edition. Englewood Cliffs, NJ: Prentice-Hall, 2000.

———. *The New Jerome Biblical Handbook.* Collegeville, MN: Liturgical Press, 1992.

Brown, Robert McAfee. *Unexpected News: Reading the Bible with Third World Eyes.* Philadelphia: Westminster Press, 1984.

Brueggemann, Walter. *The Bible Makes Sense.* Rev. ed. Louisville, KY: Westminster John Knox Press, 2002.

Drane, John, Ed. *Nelson's Illustrated Encyclopedia of the Bible.* Oxford, England: Lion Publishing, 1998. An illustrated, comprehensive fact-finding source that answers our most intriguing questions about the Bible.

Gilles, Anthony E. *The People of the Way: The Story Behind the New Testament.* Cincinnati: St. Anthony Messenger Press, 1984.

Girard, Robert C., edited by Larry Richards, PhD. *Life of Christ,* vols. 1 and 2, from the God's Word for the Biblically Inept series. Lancaster, PA: Starburst Publishers, 2000.

Hiesberger, Jean Marie, ed. *The Catholic Bible: Personal Study Edition.* New York: Oxford University Press, 1995. Includes five hundred pages of excellent, easy-to-understand background on each book of the Bible; New American Bible translation.

Libreria Editrice Vaticana. *Catechism of the Catholic Church.* Trans. United States Catholic Conference (USCC). Washington, DC: USCC, 1997.

McKenzie, John L. *Dictionary of the Bible.* Reprint edition. New York: Touchstone Books, 1995.
Perkins, Pheme. *Reading the New Testament: An Introduction.* Rev. ed. New York: Paulist Press, 1988.
Ralph, Margaret Nutting. *"And God Said What?" An Introduction to Biblical Literary Forms for Bible Lovers.* New York: Paulist Press, 1986.
———. *Discovering the Gospels: Four Accounts of the Good News.* New York: Paulist Press, 1990.
Rohr, Richard, and Joseph Martos. *The Great Themes of Scripture: New Testament.* Cincinnati: St. Anthony Messenger Press, 1988.
Vatican Council II. *Dogmatic Constitution on Divine Revelation (Dei Verbum).* Council document, November 18, 1965.
Whalen, W. Terry. *Alpha Teach Yourself the Bible in 24 Hours.* Indianapolis: Alpha Books, 2003.
Witherup, Ronald D. *The Bible Companion: A Handbook for Beginners.* New York: Crossroad, 1998.
Zanzig, Thomas. *Jesus of History, Christ of Faith.* Winona, MN: Saint Mary's Press, 1999.

Scripture Resources to Use with Young Adolescents

Calderone-Stewart, Lisa-Marie. *Faith Works for Junior High: Scripture- and Tradition-Based Sessions for Faith Formation.* Winona, MN: Saint Mary's Press, 1993.
Catucci, Thomas F. *Time with Jesus: Twenty Guided Meditations for Youth.* Notre Dame, IN: Ave Maria Press, 1993.
Hakowski, Maryann. *Sharing the Sunday Scriptures with Youth.* Winona, MN: Saint Mary's Press. Published in three separate volumes with the subtitles *Cycle A* (1998), *Cycle B* (1996), and *Cycle C* (1997).
Keller-Scholz, Rick, Jeannie Pomanowski, with others. *Teaching Activities Manual for "Breakthrough! The Bible for Young Catholics": An Introduction to People of Faith.* Winona, MN: Saint Mary's Press, 2006.
Koch, Carl, ed. *You Give Me the Sun: Biblical Prayers by Teenagers.* Winona, MN: Saint Mary's Press, 2000.
Marmouget, C. Rosemary. *Scripture Alive: Role-Plays for Youth.* Winona, MN: Saint Mary's Press, 1997.
O'Connell-Roussell, Sheila. *Saint Mary's Press® Essential Bible Dictionary.* Winona, MN: Saint Mary's Press, 2005.
O'Connell-Roussell, Sheila, and Terri Vorndran Nichols. Illustrated by Vicki Shuck. *Lectionary-Based Gospel Dramas for Lent and the Easter Triduum.* Winona, MN: Saint Mary's Press, 1999.

The ScriptureWalk series contains two books for young adolescents: *ScriptureWalk Junior High: Bible Themes* (Hakowski, 1999), and *ScriptureWalk Junior High: People of Promise* (Grant, 2002). Winona, MN: Saint Mary's Press, 1997.

Singer-Towns, Brian, ed. *Bringing Catholic Youth and the Bible Together: Strategies and Activities for Parishes and Schools.* Winona, MN: Saint Mary's Press, 2000.

Theisen, Michael. *Ready-to-Go Scripture Skits (That Teach Serious Stuff).* Winona, MN: Saint Mary's Press, 2004. This resource features skits about Abraham and Isaac, Samson, and those disciples who were present at Pentecost.

Scripture Resources for Young Adolescents Themselves

Auer, Jim. *Don't Read This Book!* Liguori, MO: Liguori Publications, 1996. A teenager's guide to Christian living written in a witty and imaginative style.

Brost, Corey, CSV. *Gospel Connections for Teens: Reflections for Sunday Mass, Cycle B.* Winona, MN: Saint Mary's Press, 2005.

———. *Gospel Connections for Teens: Reflections for Sunday Mass, Cycle C.* Winona, MN: Saint Mary's Press, 2006.

Cloninger, Claire and Curt. *E-Mail from God for Teens.* Tulsa, OK: Honor Books, 1999. This book uses the Scriptures in a novel way, presenting God's message as an e-mail filled with guidance to help teens deal with real-life issues.

———. *More E-Mail from God for Teens.* Tulsa, OK: Honor Books, 2000. The first version of this book was so popular that the authors wrote a sequel filled with more e-mail from God.

Covey, Sean. *Daily Reflections for Highly Effective Teens.* New York: Fireside Books, 1999. From the author of *The Seven Habits of Highly Effective Teens,* this is a book that will inspire teens to live a life filled with positive character traits.

Haas, David. *Prayers Before an Awesome God: The Psalms for Teenagers.* Winona, MN: Saint Mary's Press, 1998.

Heisberger, Jean Marie, and Maureen Gallagher. *Take Ten: Daily Bible Reflections for Teens.* Winona, MN: Saint Mary's Press, 2004.

Jenkins, Simon. *The Bible from Scratch, Catholic Edition: A Lightning Tour from Genesis to Revelation.* Winona, MN: Saint Mary's Press, 2006.

Pennock, Michael Francis. *What We Really Want to Know (Answers to 101 Questions Teens Always Ask).* Notre Dame, IN: Ave Maria Press, 1996. Teens submitted questions to their teacher in a classroom question box. This book is a collection of answers to their questions directly from Church teaching.

Shepp, Victoria. *Coyote Meets Jesus: Treasures in Folktales and Scripture.* Winona, MN: Saint Mary's Press, 2006.

Singer-Towns, Brian, ed. *Student Activity Workbook for "Breakthrough! The Bible for Young Catholics": An Introduction to People of Faith.* Winona, MN: Saint Mary's Press, 2006.

Music

Pena, Donna. *Diciembre en México.* GIA, 1994. Traditional and newly composed songs that celebrate the December Holy Days in the Mexican culture. Great music for celebrating *Las Posadas* (see chapter 1).

Pomanowski, Jeannie. *Faith with an Attitude.* Chesapeake Music Works, 2001.

———. *Prayer Warrior.* Chesapeake Music Works, 2004.

Films

The Chronicles of Narnia: The Lion, the Witch and the Wardrobe (2005, 143 minutes, rated PG).

Jesus of Nazareth (1977; 6 hours, 11minutes; not rated). This is a classic feature-length film directed by Franco Zeffirelli, packaged in a three-video set.

Appendix 2

Answer Key for *Breakthrough!* Workbook Puzzles

Introduction to the Gospels

1. A. Matthew B. Mark
   C. Luke D. John
2. Matthew
3. Mark
4. A. Matthew and Luke
   B. "This is the Good News about Jesus Christ, the Son of God."
   C. Jesus is the Word.
5. Moses received the Law on Mount Sinai.
6. Jesus heals a man with an evil spirit; Jesus heals Simon's mother-in-law; Jesus heals many people; Jesus heals a man with a skin disease.
7. Answers will vary.
8. "But these have been written in order that you may believe that Jesus is the Messiah, the Son of God, and that through your faith in him you may have life."

A Gospel Timeline

1. Jesus' Birth
2. Jesus' Baptism
3. Jesus' Ministry in Galilee
4. Jesus Chooses Apostles
5. Jesus' Entry into Jerusalem
6. Lord's Supper
7. Jesus' Arrest
8. Jesus' Crucifixion
9. Jesus' Death
10. Jesus' Resurrection

Jesus and His Family

Jesus' Baptism and Temptation

Mark 1:9–11	God said he was pleased with his Son, Jesus.
Matthew 4:1–11	We need God's words to live.
Mark 8:31–33	Peter did not understand what God expected of Jesus.
Mark 9:42–47	Jesus said that we should not lead others into sin.
Mark 10:35–45	People who are truly great are people who serve others.

Jesus and His Disciples

1. Simon, Andrew, James, John
2. Levi
3. Judas Iscariot
4. Nathanael
5. Peter
6. Philip
7. Andrew
8. James, John
9. James

Another name for Levi: Matthew—he is listed as the tax collector.

Jesus in Prayer

Fill-in words

1. ELIJAH
2. FATHER
3. APOSTLES
4. HUMBLE
5. ASK
6. PARABLE
7. EARLY
8. PRIVATE
9. PRAY
10. SON

Two names for the prayer Jesus taught us:

The Lord's Prayer

and

The Our Father

Gospel Images of Jesus

1. Word of Life
2. Only Son of God
3. Bread of Life
4. Light of the World
5. Good Shepherd
6. Resurrection and the Life
7. Vine (and we are the) Branches

The Gospel of John teaches that Jesus is the divine Son of God.

Jesus the Teacher

Scrambled Words

A. R**E**W**A**RD
B. EVE**R**YTHI**N**G
C. **T**REASUR**E**
D. **OT**HER**S**
E. **M**AT**E**RIA**L**
F. **S**PIRI**T**UAL
G. W**O**RL**D**LY
H. **P**HYS**IC**AL
I. COI**N**S

The Kingdom Of God is both present and still to come.

Jesus the Healer

Fill-in words that appear in the word search:

1. CLEAN
2. SERVANT
3. PETER
4. ROOF
5. FAITH
6. SABBATH
7. PRAYER
8. SEE
9. POWER
10. FATHER

Fill-in phrase: The healings of Jesus are a sign of the Kingdom of God.

T	R	E	Y	A	R	P	R	H	T
E	H	S	E	A	L	I	O	N	N
P	G	E	S	O	F	F	O	H	A
J	O	E	E	A	N	S	F	T	V
U	S	W	T	A	A	R	E	A	R
A	P	H	E	S	E	I	G	B	E
N	E	O	F	R	L	T	H	B	S
R	T	E	K	I	C	N	G	A	D
O	E	F	A	I	T	H	M	S	O
F	R	G	O	D	+	+	+	+	+

Jesus the Bread of Life

In Mark 6:33–44, Jesus fed . . .

				F	I	V	E				
T	H	O	U	S	A	N	D		M	E	N
	W	I	T	H		O	N	L	Y		
F	I	V	E		L	O	A	V	E	S	
A	N	D		T	W	O		F	I	S	H

In Mark 14:22–26, Jesus shared with his Apostles bread and wine, which he had blessed, and told them to . . .

E	A	T		T	H	E		B	R	E	A	D	
	W	H	I	C	H		I	S		H	I	S	
B	O	D	Y		A	N	D		D	R	I	N	K
T	H	E		W	I	N	E		W	H	I	C	H
	I	S		H	I	S		B	L	O	O	D	

Jesus the Person of Courage

In **Luke 19:37–38,** as Jesus neared Jerusalem, the crowd called him the king who comes in the name of the Lord.
In **Mark 14:35–36,** we learn that Jesus did not want to die but he wanted to do what the Father wanted him to do.
In **Matthew 26:14–16** and **Matthew 26:47–50,** we learn that Judas betrayed Jesus with a kiss.
In **Luke 22:54–62,** Peter wept bitterly after he denied Jesus.
In **John 19:16,** we learn that Pilate handed Jesus over to be crucified.

Jesus and His Suffering

Passages with editor's selected captions

Mark 15:16–20	Jesus is whipped and crowned with thorns.
Mark 15:21	Simon helps Jesus carry his cross.
Mark 15:22–28	Jesus is crucified.
Mark 15:29–36	People insult Jesus as he hangs on the cross.
Mark 15:37–41	Jesus dies.
Mark 15:42–47	Jesus is buried.

Descriptive paragraphs

Answers will vary.

The Risen Jesus

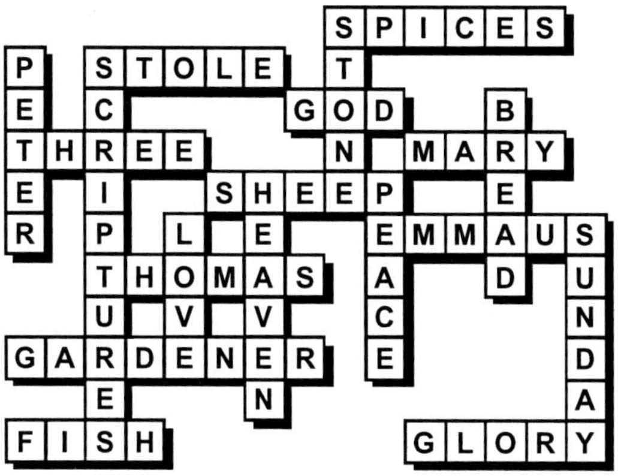

Images of Jesus in the Letters

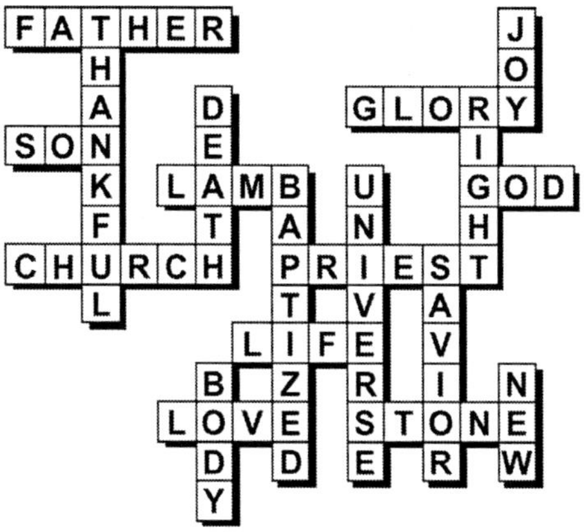

Appendix 3

Index of Activities by Chapter

Acknowledgments

The scriptural quotations contained herein are from the *Good News Bible with Deuterocanonicals / Apocrypha,* second edition. Copyright © 1992 by the American Bible Society. All rights reserved. Used with permission.

The articles on human rights on handout 1-B are from "Universal Declaration of Human Rights: All Human Rights for All," by the General Assembly, found at the United Nations' Web site, *www.un.org/Overview/rights.html,* accessed October 14, 2006. Used with permission.

The articles on the rights of children on handout 1-B are from "United Nations Convention on the Rights of the Child," November 20, 1989, found at the United Nations Treaty Collection Web site, *untreaty.un.org/English/TreatyEvent2001/index.htm,* accessed October 14, 2006. Used with permission.

The Lord's Prayer on handout 4-B is adapted from the *Sacramentary,* English translation prepared by the International Commission on English in the Liturgy (New York: Catholic Book Publishing Company, 1985), page 561. Illustrations and arrangement copyright © 1985-1974 by Catholic Book Publishing Company, New York.

The list of Scripture passages on handout 5-A is adapted from the God's Word for the Biblically Inept series, *Life of Christ,* volume 2, by Robert C. Girard and Larry Richards (Lancaster, PA: Starburst Publications, 2000), page 79. Copyright © 2000 by Starburst Publications.

To view copyright terms and conditions for Internet materials cited here, log on to the home pages for the referenced Web sites.

During this book's preparation, all citations, facts, figures, names, addresses, telephone numbers, Internet URLs, and other pieces of information cited within were verified for accuracy. The authors and Saint Mary's Press staff have made every attempt to reference current and valid sources, but we cannot guarantee the content of any source, and we are not responsible for any changes that may have occurred since our verification. If you find an error in, or have a question or concern about, any of the information or sources listed within, please contact Saint Mary's Press.